INTERVENTIONS FOR ALL

Phonological Awareness

INTERVENTIONS FOR ALL
PHONOLOGICAL AWARENESS

Yvette Zgonc

Crystal Springs SDE BOOKS

a division of Staff Development for Educators

Peterborough, New Hampshire

Published by Crystal Springs Books
A division of Staff Development for Educators (SDE)
10 Sharon Road, PO Box 500
Peterborough, NH 03458
1-800-321-0401
www.SDE.com/crystalsprings

© 2010 Yvette Zgonc
Illustrations © 2010 Crystal Springs Books

Published 2010
Printed in the United States of America
14   5

ISBN: 978-1-934026-80-9

Zgonc, Yvette.
Interventions for all : phonological awareness / Yvette Zgonc.
p. cm.
Includes bibliographical references and index.
ISBN 978-1-934026-80-9
1. Language awareness in children. 2. English language--Phonetics. 3.
Phonetics--Study and teaching (Primary) I. Title.

LB1525.6.Z45 2010
372.46'5--dc22

2010026473

Editor: Diane Lyons
Art Director and Designer: S. Dunholter
Production Coordinator: Deborah Fredericks
Illustrator: Joyce Rainville

This book is dedicated to my mother, Gertrude Gerber, whose voice of encouragement and love still resonates inside my head even though she is gone. I continue to be inspired by her 89 years of pure heart, her commitment to helping others, and her insatiable desire to learn. I miss her immensely.

This book is also dedicated to my three beautiful grandchildren—Mason, Carter, and the newest member of our family, Alexandra. Their personalities light up my life and their smiles melt my heart.

Contents

Acknowledgments

There are so many people to whom I owe an immeasurable amount of gratitude. Most instrumental has been Deborah Tapp. She approached me and initiated the idea for this book at a conference where we were both presenting. I had hoped that she'd be a coauthor, but her professional and personal obligations prevented that from happening. She did, however, contribute her expertise, as well as find four talented teachers to translate the Phonological Awareness Skills Assessment (PAST) into Spanish. They are Julester Bennett, Yasilda Stoner, Xiomara Ferrera, and Mirza Mendizabar, all from Shelby County Public Schools in Kentucky. Heartfelt thanks go to Carmen Hernandez, Ana Carrasquillo, and Cassandra Reilly who helped with some later additions.

I am forever grateful to my family. Thank you to my loving husband Frank who, after 44 years, still showers me with unconditional love and support. Many a night, he kept us fed while I typed through the dinner hour. My three sons, their wives, and my two gorgeous grandsons, Mason and Carter, each had a part in writing this book, too. They helped to revise and format forms (Thank you, Todd!), called with words of encouragement, reviewed the content, and, in the case of my grandsons, actually tried out the activities.

I also want to extend my appreciation to my brother, sister, and their spouses and families. As we've talked across the miles, they have been exceptional listeners and incredible cheerleaders.

I'd like to thank and acknowledge my colleagues and other professionals who gave their valuable time to talk or work with me on this book and support my efforts. Thank you to Linda Albert, Judy Pierce, Ann Simpson, Barrett Puschus, and Ada Berrios. I owe much gratitude to the wonderful folks at SDE and Crystal Springs Books, especially my editors, Sharon Smith and Diane Lyons. Through her incredible wit and humor, Sharon has mastered the art of how to say we need to cut more without causing me to lose my sanity. Diane worked tirelessly, providing suggestions for revisions and additions that were right on the money. In many ways, I felt she was more of a coauthor than an editor as we spent countless energizing hours on the phone brainstorming ways to enhance this book. She magically converted my ideas and words into the succinct activities you'll see in this book. These two editors became the driving force that sustained me when I was tempted to cry, "Uncle."

Introduction

Natalie Lyons awoke in a cold sweat from a recurring nightmare that she used to have a number of years ago. The scene was always the same. Her principal, Ms. Grimm, came into her classroom carrying a clipboard and taking copious notes while observing her teaching phonological awareness. After 20 minutes of this nerve-racking experience, Principal Grimm walked out of the room saying, "Mrs. Lyons, you cannot teach what you do not know." Natalie, now awake, shivered at a dream that appeared so real.

It was true. Many years ago, Natalie did not know much about phonological awareness; it had not been taught in her college courses. Now, however, because of the No Child Left Behind Act and research done by the National Reading Panel, it is a required part of the curriculum. After attending many workshops and reading books on the subject, Natalie thought she was doing a pretty good job of teaching it.

As Natalie reflected on what might have caused her to relive this nightmare after so many years, she decided that perhaps she had become too complacent. She *was* repeating the same phonological awareness activities each year. Maybe it was time to expand her repertoire. She liked the assessment she was using, but she had to admit that her interventions based on the data were not meeting the needs of all her students. In fact, now that RTI (Response to Intervention) was a requirement of her school, she often found herself struggling to find ways to teach diagnostically and differentiate instruction.

If you can identify with Natalie, then read on. You, too, might be asking yourself the following questions that made up Natalie's wish list.

1. What are some additional activities I can use to help my students succeed with all the phonological awareness (PA) skills?

2. How can I tailor these skills to work in concert with RTI?

3. Where can I find quick low to no prep-time activities that engage all students, are multimodal, and honor the multiple intelligences?

4. Where can I find a phonological awareness assessment in Spanish for my Spanish-speaking students?

Natalie decided that she was going to find the answers to her wish list, and even though she knew that the Fairy Godmother was not coming, she was determined to do what she could to enhance her students' progression on the phonological awareness skills sequence.

My ultimate wish is that this book will be the next best thing to the Fairy Godmother coming to your classroom. Having had the privilege of traveling all over the country working with and listening to countless teachers with wish lists so similar to Natalie's, it was my sincerest wish to write a book that would address these very questions.

Initially, this book was going to be an update of my earlier book, *Sounds in Action*, incorporating the basic tenets of RTI. What resulted, however, was an entirely new book.

If you're familiar with *Sounds in Action*, the background information on phonological awareness will look familiar to you, but every one of the activities here is brand new. In addition, the original Phonological Awareness Skills Test (PAST) and student progress recording forms have been revised and updated. Plus, in response to an overwhelming number of requests from teachers, I've included a Spanish-language version of the PAST. There's also a brand-new study guide for teachers.

In *Interventions for All: Phonological Awareness,* each activity is presented as an RTI tier 1, 2, or 3 lesson. Whether or not you are following RTI, I think you'll find the three-tiered model very helpful because it provides a master plan, or road map, for what to do when a student is not making progress. It offers guidelines for frequency of instruction, type of instruction, group size, and how often to assess student progress.

Although tier 2 and tier 3 instruction is more intensive and explicit, I've made every effort to differentiate instruction for all learners in all activities. You will notice that many of the activities incorporate movement for the bodily-kinesthetic learners; music and rhyme for the auditory and musical-rhythmic learners; organizing manipulatives for the tactile and logical-mathematical learners; pictures for the visual-spatial learners; and opportunities to interact for the interpersonal learners.

No matter what the modality, the goal of every activity is to keep each of your students engaged, involved, and having fun. That's when learning is sustained. Retention is more likely to occur when there is a positive emotion connected to it. So please feel free to ham it up when an activity asks you to pretend to be Dr. Goodword or a game show host; it'll help your students get more out of the activity!

If you are a brain junkie like me, you'll love the chart on pages 148 and 149, which highlights the current brain research showing that talking; thinking; reflecting; using movement, novelty, and humor; and making connections encourage learning (Politano and Paquin 2000, Sprenger 2002, and Hannaford 1995). Each activity in this book was written with that research in mind.

It is my hope that this book will clarify and concretize for you how to effectively teach phonological awareness to all of your learners. Read on to acquaint yourself with the world of phonological awareness. Then be ready to pick and choose from 96 motivational and engaging activities as you strive to help *all* your students succeed and ignite their desire to learn!

How to Use the Activities

If you have an existing phonological awareness/response to intervention (PA/RTI) repertoire, these activities will provide you with a wealth of additional choices. If your ideas account is "bankrupt," welcome to the PA/RTI bank. Here activity loans are free. There is no need to spend countless hours creating RTI activities. You get to spend your valuable time enjoying what you do best: teaching!

How Much Time Should I Spend Teaching PA?

It is recommended that kindergarten and first grade teachers teach PA 15 to 20 minutes a day to the entire class (Adams, et al. 1998) and an additional 15 to 20 minutes to those students experiencing difficulty. Second grade teachers should teach PA to the whole class for 5 to 10 minutes and to small groups or those individuals who are struggling readers for an additional 15 to 20 minutes. Of course, it is the *quality* of instruction and the *responsiveness* of the instruction to the individuals in the classroom that should be given greater consideration, rather than the amount of time expended (Yopp and Yopp 2000).

When Do I Fit PA into My Day?

A natural place to use these activities is in the language arts block. You may want to use an activity to introduce or review a skill in the "before" or "after" part of Guided Reading. These shorter lessons also function well as quick reviews of particular skills during transition times.

There Are 16 Skills. Where Do I Start?

To help you decide where to start, I suggest that you administer the Phonological Awareness Skills Test (PAST) to all of the children in your class (see pages 34 to 47). Use the data to help determine which skill(s) your students need to work on. Of course you will already be doing informal assessing of your children when you present whole-class activities in phonological awareness.

Once you determine which children need additional support beyond tier 1 activities, organize a small skills-based group and use the tier 2 activities designated for that particular skill. Monitor and assess those students to determine if they need even more support in tier 3 or if they have progressed enough to return to tier 1.

How Do Tier 1, Tier 2, and Tier 3 Activities Differ?

Tier 1 activities are considered "Universal Interventions." Use them with your whole class as part of your 90-minute language arts block or core instruction. Approximately 80 to 85 percent of students should experience success with these activities.

Tier 2 activities are considered "Targeted Interventions." They are designed for use with small, skills-based groups of homogeneous students. There should be no more than four students in a tier 2 group. The instruction for tier 2 activities is more explicit and multimodal. Students experience more frequent feedback and more opportunity to practice a skill.

Tier 3 activities are referred to as "Intensive Interventions." Instruction is generally one-on-one, and it provides more modeling, scaffolding, and practice. Instruction is slower paced, offers more cues and prompts, and has more multimodal approaches.

Can I Use a Tier 2 Activity with My Whole Class?

Although all of the activities are presented by tier level, you may choose to use them interchangeably. For example, you could use a tier 2 or 3 activity for tier 1 students; just remove some of the scaffolding. Likewise, you could adapt a tier 1 activity for use with tier 2 and 3 students. Just remember, those students will need more intensive instruction. The chart on page 16 may help you to see at a glance the differences among the three tiers.

What if I Don't Have a Book Listed in a Lesson?

Half of the activities in this book are connected to specific pieces of children's literature, both fiction and nonfiction, commonly found at elementary schools. All of the books used are cited on pages 167 and 168. But don't worry; these literature-based activities were designed so they can be used even if a particular book is not available. Although the practice words listed in the activities come from these books, you can simply use the words without the book or even change the words to connect to your own book selections.

Differences Among the Three RTI Tiers:

	Tier 1 Universal Interventions	Tier 2 Targeted Interventions	Tier 3 Intensive Interventions
Who	all students	students not making progress with tier 1 instruction (10–15%)	students not making progress with tier 2 instruction (5–10%)
Group Size	whole class	2 to 4 students	individual students
Length of Instruction	included in the daily 90-minute language arts block	an additional 20 to 30 minutes 3 to 5 times a week for 6 to 8 weeks	an additional 45 to 60 minutes per day
Type of Instruction	explicit, systematic, sequential	explicit with more practice, corrective feedback, and more multimodal opportunities	extra intensity and focus; slower paced; more cues, prompts, modeling, scaffolding, practice, and repetition; more multimodal opportunities
Recommended Monitoring	3 times a year or follow district guidelines	at least twice a month	every week or two as needed

What if I Don't Have Time to Use the Suggested Books?

Since these activities were designed so that you don't have to integrate the suggested books into the existing activity, you have choices. Feel free to use a book for your read-aloud or as your Guided Reading text and then just refer to it when teaching the lessons here. Or read just an excerpt from the featured book during the phonological awareness activity to conserve time. Please use your own judgment. You're the one who knows what will work best with your class.

Bon Voyage!

Have a wonderful trip immersing yourself in the RTI and PA connection. May this book give you the "gift of time" so that you do not have to spend hours creating skills-based activities to support your students at each tier level. Instead, you can now use your teaching time and talents to facilitate these activities and watch your children succeed.

OVERVIEW

What Is Phonological Awareness?

Phonological awareness (PA) is the understanding that our spoken language is made up of words and that our words are made up of individual units of sounds called *phonemes*. Children need to be able to manipulate these sounds in order to become fluent readers. PA skills include concept of spoken word, rhyme, syllables, phonemes, and phoneme manipulation. It's important to note that phonemes represent a skill that fits under the umbrella of PA. Phonemic awareness is also a phonological awareness skill. The terms *phonemic awareness* and *phonological awareness*, however, are often interchanged in the literature.

This subcategory of phonological awareness—phonemic awareness— is the awareness that words are composed of phonemes or sounds and that those sounds have distinct features. It involves the ability to notice, think about, or manipulate those individual sounds in words (Armbruster, et al. 2001).

Phonics is the ability to recognize the letter-sound correspondence in words. It is critical to recognize that phonological awareness is an oral skill independent of print, whereas phonics is both a visual (i.e., print) and an oral (i.e., sound) skill. Phonics and PA are inextricably woven together. Although you can have phonological awareness without phonics, you can't have phonics without phonological awareness. To distinguish between PA and phonics, try this: when you think of PA, think ears (perhaps thinking of a PA system might help); when you think of phonics, think eyes and ears. Children need solid PA training in order for phonics instruction to be effective (Blevins 1997).

In the last several decades a preponderance of evidence has revealed that phonological awareness is highly correlated to later success in reading and spelling (Adams 1990, Ehri, et al. 2001). Research also indicates that critical levels of phonological awareness can be developed through carefully planned instruction (O'Connor, et al. 1993).

Phonological awareness by itself, however, is not enough. It needs to be combined with a systematic, explicit phonics program and integrated with a literature- and language-rich environment for all students. This balanced approach to teaching reading gives students the best chance to be reading fluently by the end of third grade. Providing struggling readers with intensive PA instruction (15 to 20 minutes a day, for a total of 12 to 14 hours) has been shown to result in considerable gains (Ball and Blachman 1991, Byrne and Fielding-Barnsley 1991, 1993, 1995).

Why Is Phonological Awareness So Important?

In her book *Phonemic Awareness: Playing with Sounds to Strengthen Beginning Reading Skills* (1997), Jo Fitzpatrick states that children must be able to hear and manipulate oral sound patterns before they can relate them to print. Phonics instruction builds on a child's ability to segment and blend together sounds she hears.

In addition, our language is built on the alphabetic principle; that is, letters have names and sounds, and when these sounds are combined, they form words. PA helps children understand the alphabetic principle and enhances their ability to decode. Decoding to the point of automaticity is the first of two critical reading skills. The second is putting words together for meaning and comprehension.

Why Is Phonological Awareness So Difficult?

Why is PA so difficult for some children? Think about how children hear the words we speak. For instance, mom does not say, "Ralphie, come in and feed the /d/ /o/ /g/"; she says, "Feed the dog." She coarticulates, or blends, the sounds. It is therefore difficult for many children to hear the distinct sounds in words. Have you ever listened to two people speaking in a language that was totally foreign to you? You probably had difficulty telling how many words they said in each sentence, let alone how many phonemes were in each word.

Tips for Sounding Out Letters

Paramount to teaching PA is the ability to say the sounds of letters correctly. Many teachers who are recent college graduates have told me that learning the sounds of letters was not taught in their college courses, while veteran teachers lament that the sounds were taught, but they were taught incorrectly. If you have a speech pathologist at your school, then you have a local expert at your disposal. This person, like all speech pathologists, has known about PA for years and will be a great resource to you.

First of all, you'll notice that many of the letters in this book are surrounded by slashes. Whenever you see a letter that has a slash on either side, that means you should say the *sound* of the letter, not the *name* of the letter. If you ask a child to tell you the sound of a letter and the child says the name of the letter instead, ask, "That is the name of the letter; what is the sound?"

Let's start with the sounds of three letters: /b/, /d/, and /g/. Think about the sound that begins the word *boy*. Many of us were taught to say "buh." That is incorrect. Speech pathologists will tell you that you cannot say that sound without a vowel after it, but you must de-emphasize the vowel sound, or clip it. It may help to think about how you say the sound that ends the word *club*. The same thing applies when saying the sound that begins the word *dog* and the sound that begins the word *go*. Clip them so you don't add an "uh" to these sounds.

Say the sound that begins the word *boy* while putting the first and second fingers of one hand on your voice box. You will feel a vibration. This is a *voiced* consonant sound. Do the same for the sound that begins *dog* and the sound that begins *go*. You'll notice that all three are voiced sounds. They are also called *stop sounds* because you cannot say the sounds continuously.

Now say the sound that begins the word *pet*. Is that voiced or voiceless? Put two fingers on your voice box when you say the sound. In addition, put your other hand in front of your mouth. You should not feel your vocal chords vibrate, but you should feel and hear air coming out of your mouth. This is a *voiceless, plosive* sound. You should not hear a voiced sound. Rather, it is a forceful whisper.

Try saying the sound that begins the word *kitten* and the sound that begins the word *top*. Put two fingers on your voice box and put your other hand in front of your mouth as you say each sound. What did you notice? Are these voiced or voiceless sounds? Indeed, they are voiceless, plosive sounds. You should have felt the air on your hand as you said each of them.

Another group of sounds that you should know about are *continuant* sounds, so called because you can stretch them. Examples are /m/, /n/, and, /s/. When blending sounds, it is easier to blend continuants than stop sounds. Try blending *man*: mmmmmmmaaaaaaannnnnnn. Now try blending *bat*. You cannot stretch the /b/ and /t/. Starting with continuant sounds when introducing the alphabet will help children blend words early in their acquisition of knowledge about letters and sounds.

How to Pronounce the Sample Words in This Book

You'll notice that diacritical markings have not been used when segmenting words in this book. For example, the word "plane" is segmented as /p/ /l/ /a/ /n/. Since the word always appears right next to the sounds, simply refer to the word if you are unsure of how to pronounce a vowel sound.

SAMPLE WORDS:

- plane /p/ /l/ /a/ /n/
- name /n/ /a/ /m/
- guide /g/ /i/ /d/
- meat /m/ /e/ /t/
- pile /p/ /i/ /l/
- female /f/ /e/ /m/ /a/ /l/

The 44 Sounds of English

There are 44 recognized speech sounds, or phonemes, in the English language. Below you will find them listed.

CONSONANT SOUNDS

1. /b/ (bit)
2. /d/ (dog)
3. /f/ (fat)
4. /g/ (game)
5. /h/ (hop)
6. /j/ (jump)
7. /k/ (kite)
8. /l/ (leaf)
9. /m/ (map)
10. /n/ (not)
11. /p/ (put)
12. /r/ (rake)
13. /s/ (sit)
14. /t/ (tap)
15. /v/ (vest)
16. /w/ (window)
17. /y/ (yellow)
18. /z/ (zebra)
19. /ch/ (chip)
20. /sh/ (shop)
21. /zh/ (treasure)
22. /th/ (think)
23. /th̷/ (though)
24. /hw/ (when)
25. /ng/ (king)

VOWEL SOUNDS

26. /ā/ (make)
27. /ē/ (teeth)
28. /ī/ (kite)
29. /ō/ (soap)
30. /yoo/ (cube)
31. /ă/ (dad)
32. /ĕ/ (bet)
33. /ĭ/ (sit)
34. /ŏ/ (cot)
35. /ŭ/ (hut)
36. /ə/ (ahead)
37. /â/ (air)
38. /û/ (bird)
39. /ä/ (far)
40. /ô/ (ball)
41. /oi/ (toy)
42. /ou/ (mouse)
43. /o͞o/ (soon)
44. /o͝o/ (look)

LETTER SOUNDS CHART

To help you teach students to properly pronounce each letter sound, you may want to copy this reproducible and have it handy as a quick reference sheet.

Stop Sounds (Voiced)	b, d, g, j
Stop Sounds (Voiceless)	h, k, p, t
Continuant Sounds (Voiced)	a, e, i, l, m, n, o, r, u, v, w, y, z
Continuant Sounds (Voiceless)	f, s
Letters Taking on Other Sounds	c = /k/ or /s/ can, city qu = /k/ /w/ quick (q generally takes on the sound of /k/ and is usually followed by a u.) x = /k/ /s/ fox

Tips on Tricky Phonemes

Below you will learn how to correctly segment words with tricky phonemes. Words with these sounds are often challenging for both teachers and students. Test your knowledge using the 10 words listed below.

Consonant blends keep their own names.

blue /b/ /l/ /oo/

stop /s/ /t/ /o/ /p/

R-controlled is one sound.

horse /h/ /or/ /s/

bird /b/ /ir/ /d/

Diphthongs are one sound.

boy /b/ /oy/

mouse /m/ /ou/ /s/

The letters *ng* represent one sound.

king /k/ /i/ /ng/

hung /h/ /u/ /ng/

Digraphs are one sound.

ship /sh/ /i/ /p/

them /th/ /e/ /m/

The letter *x* represents two sounds.

box /b/ /o/ /k/ /s/

six /s/ /i/ /k/ /s/

How many phonemes are there in these tricky words?

1. church
2. ring
3. three
4. star
5. table
6. though
7. found
8. precious
9. Florida
10. fix

Answers:

1. /ch/ /ur/ /ch/ (3)
2. /r/ /i/ /ng/ (3)
3. /th/ /r/ /e/ (3)
4. /s/ /t/ /ar/ (3)
5. /t/ /a/ /b/ /l/ (4)
6. /th/ /o/ (2)
7. /f/ /ou/ /n/ /d/ (4)
8. /p/ /r/ /e/ /sh/ /u/ /s/ (6)
9. /F/ /l/ /or/ /i/ /d/ /a/ (6)
10. /f/ /i/ /k/ /s/ (4)

Phonological Awareness Skills Sequence

Phonological awareness includes a series of skills, ranging from easy to difficult, that must eventually be acquired. The main components include the following:

Concept of Spoken Word

The ability to distinguish words in a sentence

Example: I like apples. (3 words)

Rhyme

The ability to recognize rhyme, complete rhyme, and produce rhyme

Example: Does *pick* rhyme with *stick*? (yes)

Example: Complete this rhyme:

Humpty Dumpty sat on a wall.

Humpty Dumpty had a great _____. (fall)

Example: What word or pretend word rhymes with *ball*? (call)

Syllable

The ability to blend, segment, and delete syllables

Example: *Foot* and *ball* together say *football*.

Example: Clap the word parts in *rainbow*. (2 claps)

Example: Say *cupcake* without *cake*. (cup)

Phonemes

The ability to recognize initial and final sounds in words

Example: What is the first sound in the word *dot*? (/d/)

Example: What is the last sound in the word *sun*? (/n/)

The ability to blend onset and rime

Example: What is this word? /t/ /op/ (top)

The ability to blend, segment, and delete phonemes

Example: /p/ /i/ /g/. What's the word? (pig)

Example: What are the individual sounds that you hear in *pot*? (/p/ /o/ /t/)

Example: Say *take* without /t/. (ake)

Example: Say *big* without /g/. (bi)

Phoneme Manipulation

The ability to add and/or substitute phonemes

Example: Say /it/. Now add /s/. (sit)

Example: Replace the first sound in *back* with /t/. (tack)

ASSESSMENT

Phonological Awareness Skills Test (PAST) Introduction

The Phonological Awareness Skills Test (PAST) in this book is an informal, diagnostic, individually administered assessment tool to help you determine the point of instruction for your students and monitor progress made from doing the activities you select. Because it is not a normed test, there can be flexibility in its administration. For example, you can reteach the directions as necessary or add your own word for the child to blend, segment, or delete if you want to gather additional information on a particular student.

The materials the administrator of the assessment needs include the assessment itself, a pencil, and counters or chips for the student to use for the segmentation part. If counters are not available, the student can clap the number of segments instead. The assessment is administered orally since PA has to do with the sounds of language.

When Skills Are Typically Mastered

Although children develop their PA skills at different rates, it is helpful to be aware of when specific skills are typically mastered. The following table presents a suggested time line.

Skill	Typically mastered
Concept of spoken word	Preschool/kindergarten
Rhyme recognition	Preschool/kindergarten
Rhyme completion	Preschool/kindergarten
Rhyme production	Kindergarten
Syllable blending	Kindergarten
Syllable segmentation	Kindergarten
Syllable deletion	Kindergarten
Phoneme isolation of initial sound	Kindergarten
Phoneme isolation of final sound	Kindergarten/first grade
Phoneme blending—onset and rime	First grade
Phoneme blending—all phonemes	First grade
Phoneme segmentation	First grade
Phoneme deletion of initial sound	First grade
Phoneme deletion of final sound	First grade/second grade
Adding phonemes	First grade/second grade
Phoneme substitution of initial sound	Second grade

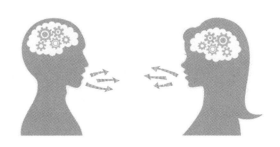

Frequently Asked Questions

Question

How fast do you say the sentences in the concept of spoken word section?

Answer

Talk in a normal conversational speed. If you tend to speak rapidly, slow it down, but speak in a natural, conversational voice.

Question

Do you administer the entire test to every child?

Answer

"Best practices" suggest that you should assess every student. However, for those students who do not appear to be struggling, you may not want to administer any of it. Be aware, though, that sometimes a student only *appears* to be doing okay. Such a child may have a good sight-word vocabulary because words in early books are almost always in a student's oral vocabulary. But once students reach the latter part of third grade, they begin to encounter many words not in their oral vocabularies, and some students then have difficulty decoding these words because of a lack of PA skills.

Start at the section where a student will have a success rate of at least five out of six correct, and go from there. You can use your judgment, based on kid watching and other school assessments, to make your decision about where to begin administering the test. If you are unsure, however, start at the beginning (concept of spoken word). Erring on the side of "too easy" when choosing where to begin the assessment is a good rule of thumb.

Question

At what point do you stop administering the assessment?

Answer

Administer the test until the child reaches a frustration level; typically, if the student misses three out of six, stop. However, use your judgment. Some children get stuck on rhyme but can do syllable blending without any problem.

Question

How many questions should a child answer correctly on each section of the assessment to be successful?

Answer

To be successful, a child needs to correctly answer at least five out of six questions, but compare the grade level of the child with the grade level at which a skill is typically mastered.

Question

What do you do with the information you get from giving the test?

Answer

Look at the first section where the child missed two or more, and use the activities in this book that relate to that section. Consider starting with tier 2 activities if the child misses skills that are supposed to be mastered at his grade level. However, follow the RTI guidelines at your school concerning decisions about placing children into tier 2 or 3 instruction. Of course, you may choose to use the tier 2 and 3 activities with students who are not mastering the PAST skills and are not yet placed in a tier 2 or 3 group for instruction.

Question

When and how often should this assessment be administered?

Answer

Consider assessing two to three times a year. The first test, or pretest, can be given in August or September. Some kindergarten teachers prefer to wait until January to give a phonological awareness assessment because of the diversity of children's home-language environments. After students experience PA instruction and activities for the first part of the year in kindergarten, it may be easier to tell who is not progressing and therefore requires intervention. Other kindergarten teachers like to get baseline data on their students and prefer to give the pretest in August.

Regardless, after the children experience whole-group and/or small-group activities relating to the assessment, it should be given in January to monitor progress. A final test, or post-test, should be given in April or May. Some teachers copy the tests on different-colored paper to help identify when the assessment was given—for instance, yellow in August, red in December, and green in April.

It is not necessary to repeat the section(s) of the test where the child scored at least five out of six correct. Each time the assessment is given again, start at the point where the child made more than one error out of six questions.

The guidelines above are appropriate for tier 1 students. Additional assessing and monitoring is necessary for tier 2 and tier 3 students. See the recommended monitoring times in the chart on page 16. Your school may have its own phonological screening instruments so you can follow those guidelines. You may also repeat sections of the PAST. Since it is an informal diagnostic tool and not one that has to be administered the same way to each student, you may want to change some of the words for successive testing so the student doesn't memorize the words. Just follow the instructions in the skill section you are assessing, but add your own words. Choose words that are about the same length or have the same number of syllables as the words provided in the test.

Question

What will I learn by assessing my Spanish-speaking students in Spanish?

Answer

Research suggests that phonological awareness skills transfer from one language to another (Durgunoglu and Oney 2000). By using the Spanish-language PAST with your Spanish-speaking students, you will learn if your students have a sense of phonological awareness in their native language. If they pass the Spanish version but fail the English PAST, then the barrier is likely a language barrier and not a phonological awareness barrier. If a student performs poorly on the PAST in his native language, then you might want to seek additional support for the student.

Question

How can I administer the Spanish-language PAST to my students if I don't speak Spanish?

Answer

Consider asking a bilingual teacher or other Spanish speaker in your district to administer the test to your Spanish-speaking students. Or perhaps you could invite a retired Spanish-speaking teacher to provide assistance.

Question

How do I find the time to give this test to my students?

Answer

There are several options. Consider having an instructional aide or volunteer work with the rest of the class while you test. Some teachers assess during sustained silent reading, while others do it while students are in flex groups or centers.

Question

What if I continue to assess the child and the child does not show adequate progress?

Answer

It is possible that the student might need to move from tier 2 to tier 3 or even need a special education referral. Another possibility is that the child is not developmentally ready to master the skill. For example, a child who cannot delete the first sound in a word is not likely to succeed at sound substitution.

Phonological Awareness Skills Test (PAST)

Name: _____ Date: _____

Teacher: _____ Grade: _____

1. CONCEPT OF SPOKEN WORD

Tell the student you are going to play a game with words and colored chips. Use the sentence "Joey likes cake" as an example. As you say each word of the sentence, push a colored chip forward—one chip per word. Then ask the child to do it. Once the student understands the skill, read each sentence to the student and ask the child to repeat the sentence while pushing up one chip for each word. Ask the student how many words are in the sentence. Put a check in the box to the right of the sentence if the child does it correctly.

1. Tom ran home.   3   ☐

2. I have two pets.   4   ☐

3. Did you eat lunch?   4   ☐

4. What are you doing?   4   ☐

5. Terry loves to play soccer. 5 ☐

6. Yesterday it rained.   3   ☐

Total: _____

2. RHYME RECOGNITION

Tell the child that two words that sound alike at the end, such as *hat* and *sat*, are rhyming words. Ask if *sit* and *bit* rhyme. (yes) Then ask if *chair* and *boy* rhyme. (no) If the child appears to grasp the skill, do the same for each of the following pairs of words. Put a check in the box to the right of the pair if the child answers correctly.

1. top - hop   yes   ☐

2. bed - said   yes   ☐

3. run - soap   no   ☐

4. hand - sand   yes   ☐

5. funny - bunny   yes   ☐

6. bat - base   no   ☐

Total: _____

3. RHYME COMPLETION

Tell the child that you are going to say a poem but need help finishing it. Read the following example and ask the child to help you complete the poem with a rhyming word. *I like to walk, I like to hike, I like to ride my big blue _____.* The child should say "bike." If the child seems to grasp the skill, do the same for the following items. Put a check in the box to the right if the child answers correctly.

1. The big bald eagle likes to fly

    So very high up in the _____.   sky   ☐

2. Our teacher said to sit up straight

    Then asked us all to count to _____.   eight   ☐

3. I saw some grapes, a whole big bunch.

    I think I'll eat them for my _____.   lunch   ☐

4. The tree outside my room is tall.

    I saw the leaves about to _____.   fall   ☐

5. My mother's ring is very old.

    It's made of silver and of _____.   gold   ☐

6. My cold is bad and getting worse.

    My teacher said to see the _____.   nurse   ☐

Total: _____

4. RHYME PRODUCTION

Tell the child that you are going to say a word. The student is to tell you a word that rhymes with it. The answer can be a real word or a nonsense word. Ask the child to tell you a word that rhymes with *sit*. Possible answers include *bit, fit, mit, pit, dit,* and *jit*. Put a check in the box to the right if the child answers correctly. Write down the child's answers on the lines provided.

1. pan _____   ☐

2. cake _____   ☐

3. hop _____   ☐

4. see _____   ☐

5. dark _____   ☐

6. candy _____   ☐

Total: _____

5. SYLLABLE BLENDING

Tell the child you are going to say a word in a funny way. The job of the student is to put the parts together and say the whole word. Give these examples, pausing between syllables: *out - side (outside), ro - bot (robot)*. Have the child say the sample words normally. Then do the following words and put a check in the box to the right if the child says them correctly.

1. pen - cil ☐   4. black - board ☐

2. rain - bow ☐   5. side - walk ☐

3. pop - corn ☐   6. pa - per ☐

Total: _____

6. SYLLABLE SEGMENTATION

Tell the student that you are going to say a word and then break it into parts, or syllables. First say, "rainbow." Then clap out the two parts in *rainbow* while saying each part. Then push up a chip as you say each syllable. Read each of the following words, and ask the child to push up a chip while saying each syllable. It is not necessary to clap the syllables again unless the skill needs to be retaught. Put a check in the box to the right if the child does it correctly.

1. sometime   2   ☐   4. fantastic   3   ☐

2. basket   2   ☐   5. maybe   2   ☐

3. bedroom   2   ☐   6. helicopter 4   ☐

Total: _____

7. SYLLABLE DELETION

Tell the student you are going to play a game with words where one part of the word is left out. For example, *sunshine* without *shine* is *sun*. Ask the child to say *airline* without *air*. The child should say, "line." Using the words below, tell the child the syllable to leave off. Use this sentence structure: "Say (*down*) *town* without *down*." Put a check in the box to the right if the student deletes the correct syllable.

1. (down)town   town   ☐   4. bas(ket)   bas   ☐

2. (in)side   side   ☐   5. af(ter)   af   ☐

3. for(get)   for   ☐   6. (skate)board board   ☐

Total: _____

Interventions for All: Phonological Awareness

8. PHONEME ISOLATION OF INITIAL SOUND

Tell the child you are going to say a word, and he is to tell you the first sound of that word. Ask the child what the first sound is in the word *top*. The child should say /t/. Do the same with the words below and put a check in the box to the right if the child says the first sound correctly.

1. big	/b/	☐	4. apple	/a/	☐
2. land	/l/	☐	5. desk	/d/	☐
3. farm	/f/	☐	6. ship	/sh/	☐

Total: _____

9. PHONEME ISOLATION OF FINAL SOUND

Tell the child you are going to say a word. The student is to tell you the last sound in the word. Ask the child what the last sound is in the word *pot*. The child should say /t/. Do the same with the words below and put a check in the box to the right if the child says the sound correctly.

1. pick	/k/	☐	4. bug	/g/	☐
2. ran	/n/	☐	5. same	/m/	☐
3. fill	/l/	☐	6. tooth	/th/	☐

Total: _____

10. PHONEME BLENDING—ONSET AND RIME

Tell the student that you are going to say some words in a funny way. The job of the student is to put the parts together and say the whole word. Do these examples by segmenting each word into onset and rime. Then have the child say the whole word blended together: /m/ /op/ is *mop*; /n/ /est/ is *nest*. Put a check in the box to the right if the child says the whole word correctly.

1. /s/ /un/	sun	☐	4. /f/ /ish/	fish	☐
2. /p/ /ig/	pig	☐	5. /ch/ /op/	chop	☐
3. /b/ /us/	bus	☐	6. /sp/ /ill/	spill	☐

Total: _____

11. PHONEME BLENDING—ALL PHONEMES

Tell the student that you are going to separate all the sounds in a word. The student is to say the whole word. Do these examples by segmenting each sound and having the student say the whole word; for example, /s/ /i/ /t/ is *sit*, and /s/ /t/ /o/ /p/ is *stop*. Read each word in segmented fashion. Put a check in the box to the right if the child says the whole word correctly.

1. /m/ /e/   me   ☐   4. /m/ /u/ /s/ /t/   must   ☐
2. /b/ /e/ /d/   bed   ☐   5. /sh/ /o/ /p/   shop   ☐
3. /h/ /a/ /t/   hat   ☐   6. /p/ /l/ /a/ /n/ /t/   plant   ☐

Total: _____

12. PHONEME SEGMENTATION

Tell the student that you're going to play a game with all the sounds in the words below. As an example, show the student the three sounds in *dime*. Push up a chip for each sound you say—/d/ /i/ /m/. Ask the child to try it with the word *hat*. Read each of the following words and ask the student to push up a chip for each sound. Put a check in the box to the right if the child does it correctly.

1. in   2   ☐   4. ship   3   ☐
2. at   2   ☐   5. sock   3   ☐
3. name   3   ☐   6. chin   3   ☐

Total: _____

13. PHONEME DELETION OF INITIAL SOUND

Tell the child you will be playing a word game where the beginning sound of a word is left off. For example, *bed* without /b/ is *ed*. Ask the child to say *fan* without /f/. The answer is *an*. Read each word below and tell the child the beginning sound to leave off. Put a check in the box to the right if the child does it correctly.

1. /s/un   un   ☐   4. /n/eck   eck   ☐
2. /p/ig   ig   ☐   5. /b/at   at   ☐
3. /m/op   op   ☐   6. /t/ape   ape   ☐

Total: _____

Interventions for All: Phonological Awareness

14. PHONEME DELETION OF FINAL SOUND

Tell the child that in this word game, the final sound of a word is left off. For example, *goat* without /t/ is *go*. Ask the child to say *meat* without /t/. The answer is *me*. Read each word and tell the child the ending sound to leave off. Put a check in the box to the right if the child does it correctly.

1. ro/d/e   row   ☐   4. sea/t/   sea   ☐

2. trai/n/   tray   ☐   5. ba/k/e   bay   ☐

3. grou/p/   grew   ☐   6. in/ch/   in   ☐

Total: _____

15. ADDING PHONEMES

Tell the child that you are going to add a sound to the beginning of a word to make a new word. For example, when /f/ is added to *an* you get *fan*. Ask the child to say /at/. Ask what you get when you add /m/. The child should say, "mat." Ask the child to do the same with the rest of the words below. Put a check in the box to the right if the child is able to blend the word correctly.

1. Say *it*. Now add /f/.   fit   ☐   4. Say *ink*. Now add /s/.   sink   ☐

2. Say *ice*. Now add /n/.   nice   ☐   5. Say *in*. Now add /ch/.   chin   ☐

3. Say *end*. Now add /b/.   bend   ☐   6. Say *top*. Now add /s/.   stop   ☐

Total: _____

16. PHONEME SUBSTITUTION OF INITIAL SOUND

Tell the child you will be playing a very different game with sounds of words. You are going to ask her to take off the first sound of a word and replace it with another sound. Example: Replace the first sound in *pail* with /m/. The new word is *mail*. Ask the child to replace the first sound in *top* with /h/. The word is *hop*. Ask the child to do the same with the rest of these words. If the child answers correctly, put a check in the box to the right.

1. Replace the first sound in *man* with /k/.   can   ☐

2. Replace the first sound in *pig* with /d/.   dig   ☐

3. Replace the first sound in *sack* with /t/.   tack   ☐

4. Replace the first sound in *well* with /f/.   fell   ☐

5. Replace the first sound in *bed* with /r/.   red   ☐

6. Replace the first sound in *shop* with /ch/.   chop   ☐

Total: _____

Phonological Awareness Skills Test (PAST) in Spanish

Name: _____ Date: _____

Teacher: _____ Grade: _____

1. CONCEPT OF SPOKEN WORD (CONCEPTO DE PALABRAS ENUNCIADAS)

Tell the student you are going to play a game with words and colored chips (say: *vamos a jugar un juego con palabras y fichas de colores*). Use the sentence "*A José le gusta el pastel*" as an example. As you say each word of the sentence, push a colored chip forward—one chip per word. Then ask the child to do it (say: *voy a decir un frase. Muéstrame cuantas palabras hay: A José le gusta el pastel*). Once the student understands the skill, read each sentence to the student and ask the child to repeat the sentence while pushing up one chip for each word. Ask the student how many words are in the sentence. Put a check in the box to the right of the sentence if the child does it correctly.

1. Yo tengo hambre.   3   ☐

2. Me gusta el pastel.   4   ☐

3. Tengo un gato negro.   4   ☐

4. Mamá compró un pan.   4   ☐

5. María juega fútbol con Juan.   5   ☐

6. Ayer llovió mucho.   3   ☐

Total: _____

2. RHYME RECOGNITION (RECONOCIMIENTO DE PALABRAS QUE RIMAN)

Tell the child that two words that sound alike at the end, such as *año* and *baño*, are rhyming words (say: *si dos palabras terminan en una manera similar, son palabras que riman*). Ask if *tío* and *mío* rhyme (say: *dime si estas palabras riman*). Then ask if *lago* and *carro* rhyme. If the child appears to grasp the skill, do the same for each of the following pairs of words. Put a check in the box to the right of the pair if the child answers correctly.

1. maleta - paleta   sí   ☐   4. juego - fuego   sí   ☐

2. piña - niña   sí   ☐   5. pato - gato   sí   ☐

3. perro - silla   no   ☐   6. mesa - coche   no   ☐

Total: _____

Interventions for All: Phonological Awareness

3. RHYME COMPLETION (TERMINACIÓN DE RIMAS)

Tell the child that you are going to say a poem but need help finishing it (say: *voy a decir un poema, pero necesito ayuda en terminarlo*). Read the following example and ask the child to help you complete the poem with a rhyming word (say: *ayúdame terminar el poema*) *Miau, miau, dice el gato, cuac, cuac, cuac, dice el _____.* The child should say "pato." If the child seems to grasp the skill, do the same for the following items. Put a check in the box to the right if the child answers correctly.

1. Veo, veo con mi ojo

   un coche que es _____ .   rojo   ☐

2. Luego voy a hacer el resto,

   Pero primero tengo que hacer todo _____.   esto   ☐

3. Es difícil tomar una siesta

   Mientras mis vecinos tienen una _____.   fiesta   ☐

4. Si quieres comprar un toro

   tienes que pagar con plata y _____ .   oro   ☐

5. ¿Quieres saber algo loco?

   Vivo en una casa hecha todo de _____ .   coco   ☐

6. Hoy hace mucho frío.

   No podemos nadar en el _____.   río   ☐

Total: _____

4. RHYME PRODUCTION (PRODUCCIÓN DE RIMAS)

Tell the child that you are going to say a word. The student is to tell you a word that rhymes with it. The answer can be a real word or a nonsense word (say: *voy a decirte una palabra, dime otra palabra que rima. Puede ser una palabra real or inventada*). Ask the child to tell you a word that rhymes with *bella* (say: *dime una palabra que rima con la palabra bella*). Possible answers include *botella, ella, zella, pella,* or *estrella*. Put a check in the box to the right if the child answers correctly. Write down the child's answers on the lines provided.

1. pato _____ ☐   4. color _____ ☐

2. mesa _____ ☐   5. piña _____ ☐

3. mio _____ ☐   6. taza _____ ☐

Total: _____

5. SYLLABLE BLENDING (COMBINANDO SÍLABAS)

Tell the child you are going to say a word in a funny way. The job of the student is to put the parts together and say the whole word (say: *vamos a decir unas palabras en una manera diferente. Vamos a decir dos partes, y luego juntarlos para formar la palabra*). Give these examples, pausing between syllables: *fue-ra (fuera), ro - pa (ropa)*. Have the child say the sample words normally. Then do the following words and put a check in the box to the right if the child says them correctly.

1. si - lla ☐   4. co - sa ☐

2. ár - bol ☐   5. pa - pel ☐

3. pas - tel ☐   6. fal - da ☐

Total: _____

6. SYLLABLE SEGMENTATION (SEPARACIÓN DE SÍLABAS)

Tell the student that you are going to say a word and then break it into parts, or syllables (say: *vas a decir una palabra y luego la dividirás en partes o sílabas*). First say, "piso." Then clap out the two parts in *piso* while saying each part. Then push up a chip as you say each syllable. Model again, if necessary, using the word *cuchara* (3). Read each of the following words, and ask the child to push up a chip while saying each syllable. It is not necessary to clap the syllables again unless the skill needs to be retaught. Put a check in the box to the right if the child does it correctly.

1. gato   2   ☐   4. ventana   3   ☐

2. casa   2   ☐   5. cama   2   ☐

3. rojo   2   ☐   6. televisor 4   ☐

Total: _____

7. SYLLABLE DELETION (BORRANDO SÍLABAS)

Tell the student you are going to play a game with words where one part of the word is left out. For example, *camisa* without *ca* is *misa* and *verdad* without *dad* is *ver* (say: *vamos a jugar un juego con palabras donde quitamos una parte de la palabra. Por ejemplo: la palabra camisa sin ca es misa y verdad sin dad es ver*). Ask the child to say *pla(to)* without *to* (say: *di pla(to) sin to*). The child should say, "pla." Using the words below, tell the child the syllable to leave off. Use this sentence structure: "*di (de)bajo sin de.*" Put a check in the box to the right if the student deletes the correct syllable.

1. (com)promiso   promiso   ☐   4. pa(to)   pa   ☐

2. (som)brilla   brilla   ☐   5. ro(pa)   ro   ☐

3. ár(bol)   ár   ☐   6. (co)mida   mida   ☐

Total: _____

8. PHONEME ISOLATION OF INITIAL SOUND (AISLAMIENTO FONÉTICO DEL SONIDO INICIAL)

Tell the child you are going to say a word, he is to tell you the first sound of that word (say: *voy a decir una palabra y vas a decirme el primer sonido*). Ask the child what the first sound is in the word *tela* (say: *¿Cuál es el primer sonido de la palabra tela?*). The child should say /t/. Do the same with the words below and put a check in the box to the right if the child says the first sound correctly.

1. gato	/g/	☐	4. mamá	/m/	☐
2. tía	/t/	☐	5. baño	/b/	☐
3. pared	/p/	☐	6. dedo	/d/	☐

Total: _____

9. PHONEME ISOLATION OF FINAL SOUND (AISLAMIENTO FONÉTICO DEL SONIDO FINAL)

Tell the child you are going to say a word. The student is to tell you the last sound in the word (say: *voy a decir una palabra y vas a decirme el último sonido*). Ask the child what the last sound is in the word *gris* (say: *¿Cuál es el último sonido de la palabra gris?*). The child should say /s/. Do the same with the words below and put a check in the box to the right if the child says the sound correctly.

1. globo	/o/	☐	4. árboles	/s/	☐
2. delicia	/a/	☐	5. muro	/o/	☐
3. lunes	/s/	☐	6. miel	/l/	☐

Total: _____

10. PHONEME BLENDING—ONSET AND RIME (COMBINACIÓN DE FONEMAS – COMIENZO Y RIMA)

Tell the student that you are going to say some words in a funny way. The job of the student is to put the parts together and say the whole word (say: *voy a decir algunas palabras en una manera diferente. Vas a juntar los partes y decir la palabra completa*). Do these examples by segmenting each word into onset and rime. Then have the child say the whole word blended together: /m/ /ano/ is *mano*; /n/ /ido/ is *nido*. Put a check in the box to the right if the child says the whole word correctly.

1. /p/ /elo/	pelo	☐	4. /p/ /ez/	pez	☐
2. /qu/ /eso/	queso	☐	5. /pl/ /uma/	pluma	☐
3. /l/ /ibro/	libro	☐	6. /ch/ /ico/	chico	☐

Total: _____

11. PHONEME BLENDING—ALL PHONEMES (COMBINACIÓN DE FONEMAS)

Tell the student that you are going to separate all the sounds in a word. The student is to say the whole word (say: *voy a separar todos los sonidos de una palabra y vas a decir la palabra completa*). Do these examples by segmenting each sound and having the student say the whole word; for example, /g/ /o/ /l/ is *gol* and /r/ /e/ /d/ is *red*.

1. /g/ /a/ /t/ /o/	gato	☐	4. /p/ /a/ /n/	pan	☐
2. /s/ /o/ /l/	sol	☐	5. /a/ /z/ /u/ /l/	azul	☐
3. /m/ /e/ /s/ /a/	mesa	☐	6. /b/ /o/ /k/ /a/	boca	☐

Total: _____

12. PHONEME SEGMENTATION (SEGMENTACIÓN DE FONEMAS)

Tell the student that you're going to play a game with all the sounds in the words below (say: *vamos a jugar un juego con algunas palabras*). As an example, show the student the three sounds in *luz*. Push up a chip for each sound you say—/l/ /u/ /z/. Ask the child to try it with the word *vaso*. Read each of the following words and ask the student to push up a chip (say: *pon una ficha*) for each sound. Put a check in the box to the right if the child does it correctly.

1. no	2	☐	4. pato	4	☐
2. cama	4	☐	5. mal	3	☐
3. sofá	4	☐	6. pez	3	☐

Total: _____

13. PHONEME DELETION OF INITIAL SOUND (FONEMAS SIN EL SONIDO INICIAL)

Tell the child you will be playing a word game where the beginning sound of a word is left off (say: *vamos a jugar un juego donde quitamos el sonido inicial de algunas palabras*). For example, *vela* without /v/ is *ela* (say: *por ejemplo, vela sin /v/ es ela*). Ask the child to say *cola* without /k/ (say: *di cola sin /k/*). The answer is *ola*. Read each word below and tell the child the beginning sound to leave off. Put a check in the box to the right if the child does it correctly.

1. /b/ año	año	☐	4. /f/ alta	alta	☐
2. /t/ ío	ío	☐	5. /d/ áme	áme	☐
3. /s/ illa	illa	☐	6. /l/ una	una	☐

Total: _____

14. PHONEME DELETION OF FINAL SOUND (FONEMAS SIN EL SONIDO FINAL)

Tell the child that in this word game, the final sound of a word is left off. For example, *frío* without the /o/ is *fri* (say: *en este juego vamos a quitar el último sonido de las palabras, por ejemplo,* frío *sin la* /o/ *es* fri). Ask the child to say sol without /l/ (say: *di* sol *sin* /l/). The answer is *so*. Read each word and tell the child the ending sound to leave off. Put a check in the box to the right if the child does it correctly.

1. ti/o/	ti	☐	4. cas/a/	cas	☐
2. taz/a/	taz	☐	5. fina/l/	fina	☐
3. limo/n/	limo	☐	6. pare/d/	pare	☐

Total: _____

15. ADDING PHONEMES (ADICIÓN DE FONEMAS)

Tell the child that you are going to add a sound to the beginning of a word to make a new word (say: *vas a añadir un sonido al principio de una palabra y hacer una nueva palabra*). Ask the child to say /año/ (say: *di* año) Ask what you get when you add /b/ (say: *¿Qué se obtiene cuando se agrega* /b/?). The child should say, "baño." Ask the child to do the same with the rest of the words below. Put a check in the box to the right if the child is able to blend the word correctly.

1. Di era. Ahora agrega /p/.	pera	☐	4. Di ola. Ahora agrega /k/.	cola	☐
2. Di alta. Ahora agrega /p/.	palta	☐	5. Di ojo. Ahora agrega /r/.	rojo	☐
3. Di ato. Ahora agrega /g/.	gato	☐	6. Di una. Ahora agrega /l/.	luna	☐

16. PHONEME SUBSTITUTION OF INITIAL SOUND (SUSTITUYENDO FONEMAS)

Tell the child you will be playing a very different game with sounds of words. You are going to ask her to take off the first sound of a word and replace it with another sound (say: *vamos a cambiar las palabras y sustituir el primer sonido por un nuevo sonido*). Example: Replace the first sound in *soy* with /d/. The new word is *doy* (say: *por ejemplo, si tengo la palabra* soy *y sustituyo el primer* /s/ *por* /d/, *hago una palabra nueva,* doy). Ask the child to replace the first sound in *pato* with /g/ (say: *cambia el primer sonido en la palabra* pato *por* /g/). The word is *gato*. Ask the child to do the same with the rest of these words. If the child answers correctly, put a check in the box to the right.

1. casa /m/	masa	☐	4. mago /l/	lago	☐
2. miel /p/	piel	☐	5. mero /p/	pero	☐
3. foto /r/	roto	☐	6. leo /f/	feo	☐

Total: _____

PAST Student Progress Report

Below each main skill are representative examples with a box next to each. Based on the PAST, put a check in the box if the child correctly answered five of the six questions on the subtest. The grade levels listed indicate when a skill is typically mastered.

Name: _____ Date: _____

Teacher: _____ Grade: _____

CONCEPT OF SPOKEN WORD

✔ The ability to distinguish spoken words in a sentence

☐ I like apples. How many words do you hear? (3) (PreK/kindergarten)

RHYME

✔ The ability to recognize, complete, and produce rhyme

☐ Does *pick* rhyme with *stick*? (yes) (PreK/kindergarten)

☐ Humpty Dumpty sat on a wall. Humpty Dumpty had a great _____. (fall) (PreK/kindergarten)

☐ What word or pretend word rhymes with *ball*? (call, tall, zall, etc.) (Kindergarten)

SYLLABLES

✔ The ability to blend, segment, and delete syllables

☐ Foot - ball—What's the word? (football) (Kindergarten)

☐ Clap the word parts in *rainbow*. (2 claps) (Kindergarten)

☐ Say *cupcake* without *cake*. (cup) (Kindergarten)

PHONEMES

✔ The ability to recognize initial and final sounds in words

☐ What is the first sound in the word *dot*? (/d/) (Kindergarten)

☐ What is the last sound in the word *sun*? (/n/) (Kindergarten/first grade)

☐ /f/ /un/ What's the word? (fun) (First grade)

Interventions for All: Phonological Awareness

✔ The ability to blend, segment, and delete initial and final phonemes

☐ /p/ /i/ /g/ What's the word? (pig) (First grade)

☐ What are the individual sounds you hear in *dot*? (/d/ /o/ /t/) (First grade)

☐ Say *take* without /t/. (ake) (First grade)

☐ Say *bug* without /g/. (bu) (First grade/second grade)

PHONEME MANIPULATION

✔ The ability to add and substitute phonemes

☐ Say *at*. Now add /b/. (bat) (First grade/second grade)

☐ Replace the first sound in *back* with /t/. (tack) (Second grade)

Teacher/Grade: _____

School Year: _____

PHONOLOGICAL AWARENESS

Indicate mastery by writing date mastery was observed to the right of the student's name and under the skill mastered.

Phonological Awareness Skills	Word	Rhyme			Syllables			Phonemes							Phoneme Manipulation	
	Concept of Spoken Word	Rhyme Recognition	Rhyme Completion	Rhyme Production	Syllable Blending	Syllable Segmentation	Syllable Deletion	Phoneme Isolation of Initial Sound	Phoneme Isolation of Final Sound	Phoneme Blending—Onset and Rime	Phoneme Blending—All Phonemes	Phoneme Segmentation	Phoneme Deletion of Initial Sound	Phoneme Deletion of Final Sound	Adding Phonemes	Phoneme Substitution of Initial Sound
	1	2	3	4	5	6	7	8	9	10	11	12	13	14	15	16
Students:	PreK/K	PreK/K	PreK/K	K	K	K	K	K	K/1	1	1	1	1	1/2	1/2	2

Note: M = Mastered = 5 out of 6 correct responses

ACTIVITIES

RTI TIER LEVEL 1

SKILL:
Concept of
Spoken Word

MATERIALS:
Ruler, aluminum
foil

Count the Words

Directions:

1. Before class cover a ruler with foil to make a conductor's baton.

2. Invite the class to sing "Happy Birthday" to the student whose birthday is the closest to the day that you are using this activity.

3. Next challenge the class to say (not sing) the entire song. (It's hard to do!)

4. Now divide the class into four groups. Have all the members of each group stand together. Assign Group 1 the word *happy*, Group 2 the word *birthday*, Group 3 the word *to*, and Group 4 the word *you*. Tell each group to say its word when you point to it with your baton.

5. Use your baton to conduct the class as they say the first line of the "Happy Birthday" song. Your students will enjoy repeating this activity several times. After each round, ask the children to tell you how many words are in the first line of the song.

6. Use this same process to have your class chorally say some short sentences, such as the samples provided. Before saying each sentence, divide the class into the correct number of groups. For example, if a sentence has five words, there should be five groups.

SAMPLE SENTENCES:

- We are a cool class. (5)
- Learning is fun. (3)
- We love to play outside. (5)
- We are so-o-o smart. (4)

RTI TIER LEVEL 1

SKILL:
Concept of Spoken Word

MATERIALS:
12 index cards, a hat or bag

LITERATURE CONNECTION OPTION:
The Very Hungry Caterpillar, by Eric Carle

Clap the Words

Directions:

1. Before class, copy the sentences below onto index cards. Put the cards into a hat or bag.

2. Read *The Very Hungry Caterpillar* to the class. After the story, tell the children that they are going to play a listening game using sentences from the story.

3. Divide the students into three teams: Team 3, Team 4, and Team 5. Instruct Team 3 to listen for sentences with three words, Team 4 to listen for sentences with four words, and Team 5 to listen for sentences with five words.

4. Demonstrate the game. Pull one card from the bag and read the sentence aloud. Let's say the card reads, "He was hungry." Ask the class to figure out how many words they heard in the sentence. Give children time to talk to their teammates. Assist the students with words that have more than one syllable. Once the answer has been given, ask the students in Team 3 (since the sentence had three words) to stand up and say the sentence while they clap each word: He (clap) was (clap) hungry (clap).

5. Continue playing until all of the cards have been read.

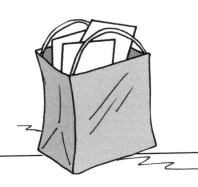

SAMPLE SENTENCES:

Three-word sentences:
- He found food.
- He was hungry.
- Fruit is good.
- He ate much.

Four-word sentences:
- The sun came up.
- The sun was warm.
- There was an egg.
- Out popped a caterpillar.

Five-word sentences:
- Each day he ate food.
- He ate through an apple.
- He built a small house.
- He turned into a butterfly.

RTI TIER LEVEL

2

SKILL:
Concept of
Spoken Word

MATERIALS:
Yellow
construction
paper

The Yellow Brick Road

Directions:

1. Before class, cut out and tape seven 5 x 8-inch yellow construction paper "bricks" to the floor or carpet to create a yellow brick road.

2. Tell the students that they are going to take a walk down the yellow brick road. (Your kinesthetic learners will especially enjoy this activity.) Clap twice. Ask a volunteer to say how many claps he heard. That student may take two steps down the road, one brick per clap. Give each child a chance to walk down the road. Be sure to vary the number of claps.

3. Tell the children that they are going to do something different now. Use the name of one of your students and say a sentence such as, "Colin likes pie." Have the student named repeat the sentence and then walk down the road, walking on one brick per word. Ask the rest of the group to tell you how many words are in the sentence. Invite another child to take a turn, and use that child's name in the next sentence. See the sample sentences for ideas.

4. Take the time to discuss with students how some words, such as *veggies* and *baseball*, have more than one word part or syllable, but they are still one word.

SAMPLE SENTENCES:

- Sarah eats ice cream. (4)
- LaMar is a good reader. (5)
- Caitlin sings like a bird. (5)
- Alexandra loves veggies. (3)
- Carter plays baseball. (3)
- Ryan and his friends play catch. (6)
- Chad rides his bike down the street. (7)

RTI TIER LEVEL

SKILL:
Concept of
Spoken Word

MATERIALS:
Fishbowl
reproducible
on page 155,
Goldfish crackers

**LITERATURE
CONNECTION
OPTION**:
*One Fish Two Fish
Red Fish Blue Fish*,
by Dr. Seuss

Disappearing Goldfish

Directions:

1. Before class make one copy of the reproducible on page 155 for each student.

2. Read the story *One Fish Two Fish Red Fish Blue Fish* to the children.

3. Give each student a copy of the fishbowl reproducible and seven Goldfish crackers. Instruct the students to arrange their Goldfish crackers in a row on the line under their fishbowls.

4. Tell the children that they will use the crackers to count the words in the sentences you read. Demonstrate using the sentence, "Some are red." Model how to count the number of words in the sentence by repeating the sentence and then sliding one Goldfish cracker into the fishbowl as you say each word. Ask students to tell you how many words are in the sentence.

5. Use sentences such as the ones provided or make up your own. After each one, ask the students to count the words in their fishbowls. Have students empty their fishbowls by sliding their crackers back down to the line before reading the next sentence.

6. To end the lesson, ask the children to pretend they are magicians and make their crackers disappear by eating them!

SAMPLE SENTENCES:

- We see them come. (4)
- We see them go. (4)
- Some are fast. (3)
- Go ask your mother. (4)
- Did you ever ride a Wump? (6)
- My name is Ned. (4)
- Where do they come from? (5)

Challenge sentence:

- I do not like my little bed. (7)

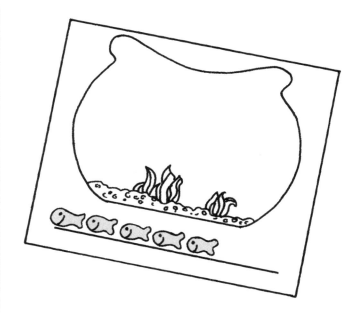

I Like Mike and I Like Sam

SKILL:
Concept of
Spoken Word

MATERIALS:
2 puppets with
movable mouths
(optional)

Directions:

1. Introduce the student to two puppets: one named Mike and one named Sam. If you don't have puppets, you can easily create an "alligator mouth" with your hands. Here's how: Hold your four fingers together and place your thumb under your pointer finger. Lift your fingers and lower your thumb to create an "open" mouth, then touch your fingers to your thumb to make a "closed" mouth. It is important to make a large movement so that the student can clearly see the mouth opening and closing. Use alternate hands for the two puppets.

2. Have the puppet named Sam say, "I like Mike."

3. Tell the child that Sam is going to say that again but this time notice what Sam's mouth does for each word. Make Sam's mouth open and close for each word so the student notices three distinct words.

4. Tell the child to place his hand under his own jaw and say, "I like Mike." Ask the child how many times his mouth opened.

5. Now have the Mike puppet say, "I like Sam." Ask the child to notice how many times Mike's mouth opened.

6. Again, have the Mike puppet say "I like Sam," and tell the child to count while Mike is saying the words. Ask the student how many words Mike said.

7. Use the puppets to illustrate three-, four-, and five-word sentences, such as the ones provided. Use all one-syllable words. Have the child count how many times the puppets' mouths open per sentence. Next, have the child repeat each sentence with his hand placed under his own jaw. After each sentence, ask the child to say how many words are in the sentence.

SAMPLE SENTENCES:

*   Sam runs fast. (3)
*   Mike drinks milk. (3)
*   Sam likes to play. (4)
*   Mike ate a pear. (4)
*   Sam and Mike swim. (4)
*   Sam and Mike have bikes. (5)

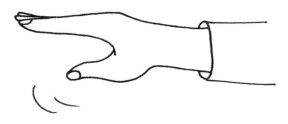

RTI TIER LEVEL

SKILL:
Concept of
Spoken Word

MATERIALS:
5 counters

**LITERATURE
CONNECTION
OPTION**:
*The Little Engine
That Could*, by
Watty Piper

I Knew You Could!

Directions:

1. Read the story *The Little Engine That Could* or tell the student about the story of the small engine who agrees to pull a long train loaded with toys over a high mountain even though other, larger engines have refused the job. Explain how the little engine has a hard time pulling the train over the mountain but keeps repeating "I-think-I-can" until it finally succeeds.

2. Give the student 5 counters, and have her place them in a row. Tell the student that you are going to say a sentence from the story. The child is to push up one counter for each word you say.

3. Say, "Chug, chug, chug." Ask the child to tell you how many "chugs" she heard. Tell her to push up one counter for each "chug" and to say the word "chug" as she pushes each counter. Say, "Puff, puff, puff." Ask the child to tell you how many "puffs" she heard. Tell her to push up one counter for each "puff" and to say the word "puff" as she pushes each counter. Repeat the procedure with the sentences provided or make up your own.

4. For reinforcement, repeat each sentence, but this time, ask the student to stomp her foot for each word. Repeat each sentence again, and ask the child to clap her hands for each word. Repeat each sentence one last time and challenge the child to come up with her own motion.

5. Celebrate the child's success and say, "I knew you could. I knew you could."

SAMPLE SENTENCES:

- The train chugged. (3)
- The train had toys. (4)
- The train was sad. (4)
- I think I can. (4)
- The little engine chugged hard. (5)

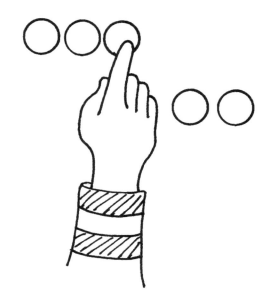

SKILL:
Rhyme
Recognition

MATERIALS:
Construction
paper, yardstick

Super Rhyming Queen

Directions:

1. Before class, make a crown from construction paper to fit your head. Write "Super Rhyming Queen" on the crown. To make a scepter, tape a paper star to a yardstick.

2. Tell the class that the Super Rhyming Queen is having trouble choosing rhyming words for her song. She needs their help! While wearing the crown and holding the scepter, sing this song to the tune of "Twinkle, Twinkle, Little Star":

   I'm the Super Rhyming Queen,
   All my words rhyme that I sing.
   I need help to write my song,
   Guess the words that don't belong.
   I'll say three, and you'll choose one.
   Pick the right one, and you're done.

3. Say three words at a time, two should rhyme but one should not. (See the sample word sets.)Tell the students that they may shout out the word that doesn't rhyme, but they must wait until you hold the scepter straight out. This gives think time to those who need it.

4. After a child correctly identifies a non-rhyming word, touch his or her shoulder with the scepter and say, "I dub you prince/princess _____." (Say the name of the child in the blank.)

5. Before moving onto the next set of words, talk about why the non-rhyming word doesn't rhyme with the other words.

SAMPLE WORD SETS:

- place, race, fat
- top, quack, shack
- add, sing, pad
- wag, flag, make
- snail, plop, whale

- song, lamp, ramp
- chill, bill, dog
- said, red, make
- red, bank, thank
- hop, hill, mop

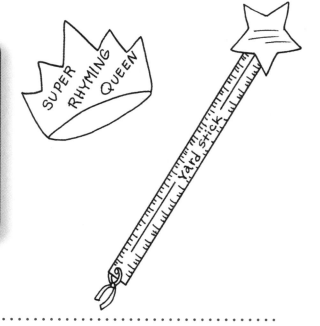

RTI TIER LEVEL 1

SKILL:
Rhyme
Recognition

MATERIALS:
3 index cards,
yarn

**LITERATURE
CONNECTION
OPTION**:
*Hooray for
Diffendoofer Day!,*
by Dr. Seuss, Jack
Prelutsky & Lane
Smith

The Diffendoofer Game

Directions:

1. Before class make three necklaces by punching two holes at the top corners of each index card and stringing yarn through the holes. Write the number 1 on one index card, the number 2 on another index card, and the number 3 on the last index card.

2. Read *Hooray for Diffendoofer Day!* to the students. Ask the students if they are ready to play a rhyming game that the students at Diffendoofer School play.

3. Choose three student volunteers to be "contestants" in the game. Instruct the students to come up to the front of the class and stand shoulder to shoulder. Place a chair behind each student and give the students each a necklace to wear.

4. Whisper one word into each student's ear. Two of the words should rhyme and one should not. For example, whisper the word *name* to Contestant Number 1, the word *same* to Contestant Number 2, and the word *cake* to Contestant Number 3.

5. Instruct the contestants to call out their words when you say their numbers. After all three students have said their words, the other students in your class must decide which student has the non-rhyming word and is the "Diffendoofer." Tell students when they think they know the answer they should hold up one, two, or three fingers to indicate which person is the Diffendoofer. The Diffendoofer must then sit down.

6. If the Diffendoofer can explain why he had to sit down (his word didn't have the same chunk of sound at the end), then he may stand up and the class shouts, "Hooray! Hooray!" After each round, invite three new contestants up to play. Use the word sets provided, or create your own.

SAMPLE WORD SETS:

- name, same, why
- test, song, best
- noodles, gift, poodles
- how, park, bark
- noise, boys, ball

- hard, how, yard
- ditch, such, much
- candle, arrow, handle
- flea, me, flip
- tomato, apple, potato

2

RTI TIER LEVEL

SKILL:
Rhyme
Recognition

MATERIALS:
None

You're Out!

Directions:

1. Review the definition of rhyming words. Explain that all words with the same chunk of sound at the end will rhyme. Point out that /ack/ is the chunk of sound that makes the words *back, sack,* and *pack* rhyme.

2. Tell the children that they are going to be umpires at a baseball rhyming game. You will be the pitcher and throw them three words at a time. Two of the words will rhyme. One word will not rhyme. When they hear the non-rhyming word, they should repeat the word followed by, "You're out!" At the same time, they should make the physical sign for an out that a real baseball umpire makes: the arm is bent, thumb up, and the arm moves like a hitchhiker's.

3. Give them an example. Pitch out the words *hit, sit,* and *fan.* The umpire says, "Fan, you're out!" while performing the hand signal for an out.

4. Talk about why the word *fan* is out. It doesn't rhyme with *hit* and *sit* because it has a different chunk of sound at the end. *Hit* and *sit* end with /it/ and *fan* ends with /an/.

5. Give each student several turns to be the umpire. Remind the umpire to tell the group why the word is out each time. Use the word sets provided, and add more of your own.

SAMPLE WORD SETS:

- sit, stop, fit
- bet, set, up
- still, rang, clang
- never, clever, table

- rope, desk, soap
- hat, corn, horn
- dog, pig, frog
- phone, star, car

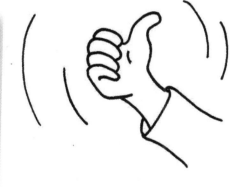

RTI TIER LEVEL

SKILL:
Rhyme
Recognition

MATERIALS:
None

**LITERATURE
CONNECTION
OPTION**:
*Bringing the Rain
to Kapiti Plain*, by
Verna Aardema

Rain on Kapiti Plain

Directions:

1. Review the definition of rhyming words. Tell the children that words that sound alike at the end, such as *cake, bake*, and *lake*, rhyme because they all end with the sound chunk /ake/.

2. Read the cumulative nursery rhyme *Bringing the Rain to Kapiti Plain* to the children. Tell them to listen for all of the rhyming words. Point out how the rhymes build on each other. (If they are familiar with *The House that Jack Built*, you may want to compare the two stories.)

3. Tell the students that they are going to play a listening game. Say, "Close your eyes. I will make two sounds; if you think the sounds are the same, you should raise your hand. If you think that they are different, you should cross your arms." Make two sounds. For example, clap twice (the students should raise their hands). For the next one do a fake sneeze and then tap a pencil (students should cross their arms.) Perform two or three more examples.

4. Tell the students that now they are going to play a word game. You will read some words from the story (see the samples provided). If they think the words rhyme, they should make a sun by putting up both arms with their fingers touching to form a circle. Ask students to explain why the words rhyme.

5. If the two words do not rhyme, the students should put both arms up in the air and then slowly lower them while moving their fingers as if it is raining. Ask students to tell why the words don't rhyme. (The words don't have the same chunk of sound at the end.)

SAMPLE WORD SETS:

- drought - about
- rain - plain
- dry - wet
- dry - sky

- cloud - ground
- bird - boy
- herd - bird
- feather - weather

RTI TIER LEVEL

SKILL:
Rhyme
Recognition

MATERIALS:
Jail reproducible
on page 156,
3 counters

Rhymenappers

Directions:

1. Before class make a copy of the reproducible on page 156.

2. Tell the child that some non-rhyming words are sneaking into Rhyming Town to "rhymenap" some words for ransom. The student's job is to figure out which one of the words is the rhymenapper and put it behind bars.

3. Review the definition of rhyming words. Tell the child that words that sound alike at the end, such as *hat, pat*, and *sat*, are rhyming words because they all end with the sound chunk /at/.

4. Give the student the jail reproducible and three counters. Have the child put the counters on the line under the jail. Each counter will represent one of the words you say.

5. Demonstrate with an example. Say, "Pen, hen, top." As you call out each word, have the student touch one counter at a time. After you finish saying the words, point to the first counter and ask the student to tell you which word that counter represents (pen). Point to the middle counter and ask the student to tell you what word that counter represents (hen). Point to the last counter and ask the student to tell you which word that counter represents (top).

6. Ask the student to figure out which word is the rhymenapper—the one that does not rhyme with the others. Instruct the student to take the counter that represents the non-rhyming word and push it up behind bars. Ask the child to explain why the word *top* had to go to jail (because it doesn't rhyme with *pen* and *hen*.) Once finished say, "Clear the jail!" and begin again. Use the sample word sets or make up your own.

SAMPLE WORD SETS:

- man, van, lit
- rack, pet, sack
- boat, goat, ant
- mat, fun, run
- rug, tug, now
- mop, sit, fit

RTI TIER LEVEL

SKILL:
Rhyme
Recognition

MATERIALS:
Craft stick, red
construction
paper

**LITERATURE
CONNECTION
OPTION**:
*Oh, How I Wished
I Could Read!*, by
John Gile

Hey Diddle, Diddle

Directions:

1. Before class cut three 3 x 3-inch squares from red construction paper.

2. Read *Oh, How I Wished I Could Read* to the student. Tell the child to listen for the rhyming words. Remind the student that rhyming words will all have the same chunk of sound at the end. Point out that the words *bet, pet*, and *set* rhyme because they all end with the sound chunk /et/.

3. Read this poem to the child:

   Hey diddle, diddle, can you figure out the riddle?
   Which is the word that doesn't fit?
   Is it word number one, or word number two,
   Or word number three that takes the hit?

4. Put three red squares down. Give the student a craft stick. Point to the first square and tell the child it stands for the word *deep*. Have the child say the word *deep*. Point to the second square and tell the child it stands for the word *sad*. Have the child repeat the word *sad*. Use the same process for the third square saying the word *had*. You touch each square and repeat the words, then ask the child to use the craft stick to hit the square representing the word that doesn't rhyme. Ask the child to explain why the word doesn't rhyme. (The word doesn't have the same chunk of sound at the end.) Continue in this manner using the sample list of words provided, or make up your own words. Be sure to read the poem before each set.

SAMPLE WORD SETS:

- ring, pot, dot
- old, name, fold
- feet, street, fence
- tree, gate, bee
- bus, stop, mop
- cat, sign, line
- floor, door, dog

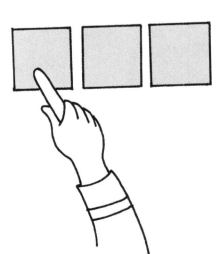

SKILL:
Rhyme
Completion

MATERIALS:
None

Pat Your Back

Directions:

1. Tell the class that they are going to play a rhyming game. Partner up the students. Explain that you will read a short poem, but you'll leave off the last rhyming word. When a pair thinks it has the rhyming word that completes the poem, the partners should raise their hands. Try this example together:

   ➤ I like to eat some chocolate cake.
   I don't like hissing like a _____. (snake)

2. Read these couplets. Have fun making up more of your own. Accept any word that rhymes, including silly words. After the last couplet, have the students call out the answer and pat their backs.

   ➤ I like to look at my green plant.
   I don't like stepping on an _____. (ant)

   ➤ I like to fill a grocery bag.
   I don't like shirts that have a _____. (tag)

   ➤ I like to take some great big sips.
   But I don't like to burn my _____. (lips)

   ➤ I like to travel with no fuss.
   But I don't like to ride a _____. (bus)

   ➤ I like to use my brain and think.
   But I don't like to clean the _____. (sink)

   ➤ I like to see a running mouse.
   I don't like mice inside the _____. (house)

   ➤ You all worked hard to stay on track.
   And now it's time to pat your _____. (back)

3. To add engagement to the activity, each time a pair gives a correct answer draw a part of a stick figure person on the board. When the first pair thinks of a rhyming word, draw the head. When the second pair thinks of a rhyming word for the next couplet, draw the neck. Continue in this manner until the entire stick figure is drawn.

SKILL:
Rhyme
Completion

MATERIALS:
None

**LITERATURE
CONNECTION
OPTION**:
*The Fourth Little
Pig*, by Teresa
Celsi

Daring Pig Four

Directions:

1. Quickly review the original story of *The Three Little Pigs*. Tell the class that you are going to read a different version of the story. Read *The Fourth Little Pig*. Ask the students to listen for the rhyming words.

2. Explain that the fourth little pig liked to play rhyming jokes on her brothers by ending rhymes in a silly way. Invite the children to play the fourth little pig's rhyming game.

3. Divide the students into groups of four. Read the first rhyme below and tell the groups to put their heads together to figure out the correct ending word. When they think they have it, instruct them to stand quietly and wait to be called on.

4. Here are the fourth little pig's silly rhymes. Place emphasis on the first rhyming word and pause before you say the incorrect word that doesn't rhyme. Congratulate the groups as they figure out each riddle.

> ➤   A long time ago, there were three little *pigs*
>   With homes made of bricks and of straw and of . . . macaroni. (twigs)

> ➤   Their sister, the bold and the daring Pig *Four*
>   Stopped by to visit and knocked on their . . . toes. (door)

> ➤   The door opened a crack, then it opened up *wide*.
>   "Get in," said the boys, "There are bad wolves . . . typing. (outside)

> ➤   "You can't spend your whole life just sitting and *shaking*.
>   There are places to see and things to be . . . tickled. (making)

> ➤   "You're hopeless!" their sister cried out with a *frown*.
>   Then she huffed and she puffed and she blew their house . . . up. (down)

SKILL:
Rhyme
Completion

MATERIALS:
Ruler, aluminum
foil

Down by the Bay

Directions:

1. Before class make a "rhyming stick" by covering the ruler with foil.

2. Tell the students that they are going to sing a song to practice their rhyming skills. Show them the rhyming stick. Tell them that when you pass the stick to them it will be their turn to think of a rhyme for the song.

3. Sing the traditional children's song "Down by the Bay." Invite your students to join in. When you get to the verse that begins, "Did you ever see a _____," choose a verse from the ones provided and sing the entire line except for the very last word. Pass the rhyming stick to a student and ask her to complete the verse. For example, if you say, "Did you ever see a *cat* wearing a _____?" the student would say "hat." You should accept any word that rhymes, even if it's a silly word.

Down by the bay
Where the watermelons grow,
Back to my home
I dare not go.
For if I do,
My mother will say
Did you ever see a _____
Down by the bay?

SAMPLE SONG VERSES:

- Did you ever see a *cat* wearing a _____ (hat)
- Did you ever see a *goat* rowing a _____ (boat)
- Did you ever see a *fox* sitting on a _____ (box)
- Did you ever see a *pig* wearing a _____ (wig)
- Did you ever see a *fly* wearing a _____ (tie)
- Did you ever see a *ghost* eating some _____ (toast)
- Did you ever see a *mouse* painting a _____ (house)
- Did you ever see a *bear* combing his _____ (hair)
- Did you ever see a *frog* walking his _____ (dog)
- Did you ever see a *moose* kissing a _____ (goose)

RTI TIER LEVEL

SKILL:
Rhyme
Completion

MATERIALS:
None

**LITERATURE
CONNECTION
OPTION**:
Madeline,
by Ludwig
Bemelmans

Rhyme Time

Directions:

1. Read the story *Madeline* to the children. After you finish reading the story, tell the children that Madeline's friends were going to visit Madeline in the hospital the next day. They were so excited about seeing her that they couldn't go to sleep. They invented a rhyming game to play, in which one person started a very short rhyme and another person had to finish it. Let's play their game.

2. Partner up the students. Explain to the class that you will read the first part of the rhyme and the partners must put their heads together to come up with a rhyming word to finish it. When a pair thinks it has an answer, the partners should raise their hands.

3. Before starting the activity, provide this think-aloud example. Touch your head and strike a "thinking" pose. Say, "There was a great big *cat* who wore a funny . . . hmmm, what rhymes with *cat*? Could it be *coat*? No, *coat* doesn't rhyme with *cat*. How about *hat*? There was a great big cat who wore a funny hat. Yes! Now, why do you suppose that works? (If necessary, explain that *cat* and *hat* both end with the same chunk of sound.) Are you ready to try some with your partner?"

4. Read the rhymes below. Place emphasis on the first rhyming word so the children will know which word to rhyme. Tell the group that some of the rhymes are very silly! You should accept any word that rhymes, even if it's a made-up word.

   ➤ There were *vines* in straight _____. (lines)

   ➤ There was a *mouse* in the _____. (house)

   ➤ She turned on the *light* in the middle of the _____. (night)

   ➤ She told a *lie* and started to _____. (cry)

   ➤ I saw a *frog* talk to a _____. (dog)

   ➤ He bought a *pickle* for a _____. (nickel)

   ➤ Look at the *fox* sitting in the _____. (box)

   ➤ I saw a *giraffe* who started to _____. (laugh)

   ➤ I saw Danny *spit* on his catcher's _____. (mitt)

   ➤ Sarah ate her ice cream *cone* while she was talking on the _____. (phone)

   ➤ Can you believe a big *baboon* was eating with a fork and _____? (spoon)

SKILL:
Rhyme
Completion

MATERIALS:
Reproducible on
page 157

I'm Thinking of a Word

Directions:

1. Before class, copy the reproducible on page 157 and cut out the rhyming word pictures.

2. Give the student the rhyming word pictures and ask him to place them in a row on the table. Ask the student to say the name of each picture (provide assistance if necessary).

3. Tell the student you are going to read some rhyming poems, but the last word in each poem is missing. He must find the picture that completes the rhyme.

4. Read the rhymes below. Put emphasis on the first rhyming word so the child will know which word to rhyme.

➤ I'm thinking of a word.
It rhymes with *dot*.
It's used for cooking food.
The word is _____. (pot)

➤ I'm thinking of a word.
It rhymes with *dish*.
It swims under water.
The word is _____. (fish)

➤ I'm thinking of a word.
It rhymes with *rope*.
It washes off dirt.
The word is _____. (soap)

➤ I'm thinking of a word.
It rhymes with *tree*.
It unlocks a door.
The word is _____. (key)

➤ I'm thinking of a word.
It rhymes with *boat*.
You wear it when it's cold.
The word is _____. (coat)

➤ I'm thinking of a word.
It rhymes with *frog*.
It likes to bark.
The word is _____. (dog)

RTI TIER LEVEL

SKILL:
Rhyme
Completion

MATERIALS:
None

**LITERATURE
CONNECTION
OPTION**: *When
the Teacher Isn't
Looking And
Other Funny
School Poems*, by
Kenn Nesbitt

Clap, Clap, Plop

Directions:

1. Teach the child the following game. Clap your hands twice and then hit your thighs with both palms on the third beat. As you make the action for each beat, assign each beat a word: clap, clap, plop. Pause after touching your thighs before starting the next series. Repeat. For the third repetition, leave out the beat on your thighs and ask the child to show you and tell you what beat was left out. The child should put her hands on her thighs and say, "Plop." Repeat the entire process to make sure the child understands the game. Scaffold as much as needed.

2. Try some new patterns. Let the child guess the last sound and action.

   Clap, Plop, Clap; Clap, Plop, Clap; Clap, Plop, _____. (Clap)
   Clap, Plop, Plop; Clap, Plop, Plop; Clap, Plop, _____. (Plop)
   Plop, Clap, Clap; Plop, Clap, Clap; Plop, Clap, _____. (Clap)

3. Tell the child that just as she figured out the patterns in the clapping game, she can also figure out the ending words in many poems—even if she hasn't heard them before—because there is a rhyming pattern. Read the short rhymes below. Put emphasis on the first rhyming word so the child will know which word to rhyme. If the child struggles, give her a choice of two words, one that rhymes and one that doesn't rhyme.

   ➤ One, two, three; one, two, three
      Mrs. Neuman drank some _____. (tea)

   ➤ Two, three, four; two, three, four
      Mr. Bumpkin shut the _____. (door)

   ➤ Three, four, five; three, four, five
      Honeybees went to their _____. (hive)

4. Read several poems from *When the Teacher Isn't Looking And Other Funny School Poems* or a poem book of choice, and ask the student to identify the rhyming words in each poem.

RTI TIER LEVEL

SKILL:
Rhyme
Production

MATERIALS:
none

Silly Simon Says

Directions:

1. Review the rules for the game Simon Says with your class. As a warm-up activity, you may want to play one quick round of Simon Says. (Stop playing after giving the first command that Simon doesn't say.)

2. Tell the class that now they will play a game called Silly Simon Says. Explain that it's called Silly Simon Says because Simon uses silly rhyming words that rhyme with real body parts. They must figure out what body part rhymes with Simon's silly rhyming word first and then touch that body part.

3. Give commands such as the ones below. Place emphasis on the silly word. Allow the class some "think time" before asking them to call out the answer. As soon as the correct word is said, students may do the action —but only if "Simon says" of course!

   ➤ Simon says touch your *belbow*,
     What he means is touch your _____. (elbow)

   ➤ Simon says touch your *care*,
     What he means is touch your _____. (hair)

   ➤ Simon says touch your *flea*,
     What he means is touch your _____. (knee)

   ➤ Simon says touch your *hose*,
     What he means is touch your _____. (nose or toes)

   ➤ Simon says touch your *mummy*,
     What he means is touch your _____. (tummy)

   ➤ Touch your *marm*,
     What he means is touch your _____. (arm)

   ➤ Simon says touch your *zears*,
     What he means is touch your_____. (ears)

   ➤ Simon says touch your *sand*,
     What he means is touch your _____. (hand)

4. Continue playing as long as the interest is high.

RTI TIER LEVEL

1

SKILL:
Rhyme Production

MATERIALS:
None

LITERATURE CONNECTION OPTION:
The Hungry Thing, by Jan Slepian & Jan Seidler

The Hungry Thing

Directions:

1. Read *The Hungry Thing* to your students. In this story a monster asks for food in a silly way that the grown-ups in the town have a hard time understanding. They wonder, what are shmancakes, tickles, feetloaf, hookies, and gollipops? A little boy in the town figures it out. The monster wants pancakes, pickles, meatloaf, cookies, and lollipops!

2. Tell the children that the Hungry Thing needs their help to make a shopping list.

3. Say the name of a food from the sample shopping list provided. Ask students to think of how the Hungry Thing might say that word. Their responses should be silly, nonsense words, but they must rhyme with your word. Accept several ideas before reading off the next item on the list.

4. Jot down a few of the students' responses for each of the items. Do not let the students see your list. You will use it for the closing part of this activity.

5. When the students are done, read the silly words back to them and see if they can come up with the real words.

SAMPLE SHOPPING LIST:

- applesauce
- cupcakes
- meatballs
- pudding
- popsicles
- ice cream
- waffles
- broccoli
- cucumbers
- celery
- hamburgers

RTI TIER LEVEL

SKILL:
Rhyme
Production

MATERIALS:
1 die, deck of
playing cards

Roll a Rhyme

Directions:

1. Review the definition of rhyming words. Explain that all words with the same chunk of sound at the end will rhyme. Point out that /ig/ is the chunk of sound that makes the words *big, dig*, and *pig* rhyme.

2. Have the students sit in a circle. Tell the students they will play a rhyming game using a die. Ask one student to be the leader. Have the leader roll the die. Starting with the leader and going clockwise around the circle, ask everyone to say a word that rhymes with the number that was rolled.

3. For example, if a four came up, students could say words such as *door, more, pour*, and *floor*. (The chunk of sound at the end of the word does not have to be spelled the same way; it only needs to sound the same.) If a person cannot think of a real word to rhyme with the number rolled, a silly word or nonsense word is acceptable. For example, if the number two was rolled, a student could say "shmoo."

4. Continue playing in this manner until each student has a turn to be the leader.

5. Try this activity next. Pull any five cards from a deck of playing cards. Fan the cards and hold them in your hand face down. In turn, invite each child to choose a card. The child says the name of the number or picture on the card. Tell the student to say a word that rhymes with that number or picture. For example, if she pulls a queen, she could say "mean." Accept silly words as long as they rhyme.

Interventions for All: Phonological Awareness

RTI TIER LEVEL

SKILL:
Rhyme
Production

MATERIALS:
None

**LITERATURE
CONNECTION
OPTION**:
Zoo-Looking, by
Mem Fox

High Five!

Directions:

1. Review the definition of rhyming words. Explain that all words with the same chunk of sound at the end will rhyme. Point out that the words *sit, hit*, and *fit* rhyme because they end with the sound chunk /it/.

2. Read *Zoo-Looking* to the children and ask them to listen for the rhyming words. (All of the rhyming words in this story share the sound chunk /ack/). Tell students that you are going to reread the story so they can figure out what the rhyming chunk is. Tell them to touch their ears as soon as they figure it out. When most of the students are touching their ears, ask them to say the rhyming chunk. (/ack/)

3. Tell the students they will play a game called High Five. Choose a rhyming chunk, such as /ill/. Hold up your hand with a closed fist. Ask students to call out words with the /ill/ chunk at the end. Each time a rhyming word is said (nonsense words are acceptable), put up one finger; continue until you've extended all five fingers. Now give each student a high five and congratulate them for working together to think up so many rhyming words. Play the game several more times, using a different rhyming chunk for each new round.

4. Arrange the students in a circle to play the next game. Choose a rhyming chunk such as /ate/. Say a word that rhymes with /ate/ and toss the beanbag to a student. That student must say a word that rhymes with /ate/ and toss the beanbag to another student. Continue playing until each student has had a turn. Compliment them on their good rhyming skills. Play again with a different rhyming chunk.

SAMPLE RHYMING CHUNKS:

- /ar/
- /an/
- /eat/
- /end/
- /ink/

- /ip/
- /ot/
- /op/
- /un/
- /ump/

RTI TIER LEVEL

SKILL:
Rhyme
Production

MATERIALS:
Reproducible on
page 158,
9 counters

Rhymo!

Directions:

1. Before class, make two copies of the reproducible on page 158. Cut the pictures out of one copy. Use the other copy as the game board.

2. Tell the student that he will be playing a game called Rhymo. Give the student the game board and nine counters.

3. Place the cut out pictures in a stack, face down, on the table. To play, the student picks the top card and names the picture. The student must think of and say a word that rhymes with the picture. Then the student names the picture again and places a counter over that picture on his game board.

4. For example, if the student chooses the picture of the flag he could say, "flag-bag-flag," and place a counter on his game board over the picture of the flag. Accept nonsense words as long as they rhyme with the words pictured on the cards.

5. When the student gets three counters in a row, he calls out, "Rhymo!" Play several rounds, using different rhyming words if the same picture is chosen again.

RTI TIER LEVEL

SKILL:
Rhyme
Production

MATERIALS:
Construction
paper

**LITERATURE
CONNECTION
OPTION**:
*Rhyming Dust
Bunnies*, by Jan
Thomas

Put on Your Thinking Cap

Directions:

1. Before class, make a headband from construction paper to fit your student's head. Write the words "Thinking Cap" on the headband.

2. Read *Rhyming Dust Bunnies* to your student. Teachers and students delight in this silly book about Ed, Ned, and Ted, who rhyme all the time, and Bob who does not.

3. Tell the student that today she gets to be an expert rhymer because she is going to use her thinking cap to help her think of words that rhyme with the words you say.

4. Give the student an example. Say the word *red*. Tell the student that you are going to think really hard inside your head to come up with a word that rhymes with the word *red*. Put your finger up to your head in a "thinking" pose. Then say the word *bed*. Ask the student if *red* rhymes with *bed*. Then ask the student to think of other words that rhyme with the word *red*.

5. Put the Thinking Cap headband on the student. Say a word from the list provided, or make up your own. Ask the student to think of as many words as she can that rhyme with your word. Silly words are acceptable as long as they rhyme with your word.

6. When the student has exhausted her words, give her a new word.

SAMPLE WORDS:

- hat
- rake
- sack
- lip
- pill
- ink
- met
- feet

- bet
- hop
- boat
- cold

Challenge words:

- bunny
- rumble
- flute

RTI TIER LEVEL 1

SKILL:
Syllable Blending

MATERIALS:
None

Guess Who?

Directions:

1. Tell the class that they are going to play a fun guessing game called Guess Who.

2. Explain that you will say one of their names in a very strange way. You are going to stretch it out by syllables. They have to guess whose name you are saying. Once they figure it out, they should point to that student.

3. Give the students an example: "If I were saying the name LaToya, I would stretch it out like this: La-Toy-a. Now, everyone point to LaToya." After all of the children are pointing to LaToya, she must stand up and say her name in the normal way.

4. Repeat the activity five or six more times. Use names with at least two syllables. Each time the class identifies the person, invite that person to stand up and say his or her name normally.

5. Next, partner the students and tell them to sit facing each other, "eye-to-eye and knee-to-knee." Challenge them to figure out the words you say. Tell them that the words will be silly made-up words that you are going to stretch out. Say one silly word at a time from the list provided, syllable by syllable, and then ask a pair to tell you how to say the word blended together.

6. Tell the children that the pair who figure out this last word get their names on the board under the $64,000 word: *su-per-cal-i-frag-i–lis-tic-ex-pi-al-i-do-cious*.

SAMPLE SILLY WORDS:

- fan - lap - ster
- kin - pen - dip
- fly - chot
- pay - dle - roo
- doo - bee - dop
- shun - go
- mid - lee - bop
- wik - e - sit
- sip - tap - ly

1

SKILL:
Syllable Blending

MATERIALS:
None

LITERATURE CONNECTION OPTION:
The Great Kapok Tree, by Lynne Cherry

The Great Kapok Tree

Directions:

1. Read *The Great Kapok Tree* to the children. After the story, ask the students to try to name all of the animals in the story who were trying to tell the sleeping man not to chop down the tree.

2. Tell the students that they will play a game. In the game, the sleeping man is having a dream about the animals. He is trying to name them, but in his dream their names are all stretched out. Invite the children to listen to the stretched-out names and see if they can figure them out.

3. Demonstrate with the word *tiger*. Put one finger on your chin and say, "ti," and then put a second finger on your chin and say, "ger." Have the students copy you. Call on one student to put the parts together and say the animal's name in the normal way. (Show students how to place additional fingers on their chins for words with more than two syllables.)

4. Continue in this manner using the names of the animals provided on the list. Invite students to name other animals and continue the game.

ANIMAL NAMES:

- tou - can
- ja - guar
- por - cu - pine
- ant - eat - er
- ti - ger
- le - mur
- par - rot
- go - ril - la
- gib - bon

Challenge words:

- but - ter - fly
- cap - y - bar - a
- bo - a - con - stric-tor
(They will have to add their thumbs to this one!)

ti-ger

SKILL:
Syllable Blending

MATERIALS:
2 paper lunch
bags, orange
and white
construction
paper

What's a Raincorn?

Directions:

1. Before class make two puppets named Pumpkinface and Moonpie. Cut out a pumpkin shape from orange construction paper and a full moon shape from white construction paper. Glue each cut-out to the bottom of a small paper lunch bag and add facial features with a marker.

2. Introduce Pumpkinface and Moonpie to your students. Tell them that these two friends created the coolest syllable game while out at recess today. They decided to mix up compound words and come up with funny, brand-new words.

3. Have Pumpkinface say to Moonpie, "What if I took the *cup* from *cupcake* and the *ball* from *eyeball* and put them together?" Have Moonpie say, "I know. I know. It would be *cupball*." Then have both puppets laugh. Have Moonpie say, "It's my turn now. What if I took the *fire* from *fireplace* and the *dog* from *bulldog* and put them together? Let's see, I would have *fire* and *dog*." This time, have the students guess the new word. (firedog)

4. Have Pumpkinface say, "Hey, I have an idea. Girls and boys, would you like to play with us?" Have Moonpie say, "Yeah! That sounds like fun. Are you ready?"

5. Make Pumpkinface say, "What if I took the *rain* from *rainbow*?" Have Moonpie continue, "And I took *corn* from *popcorn*?" Have Pumpkinface say, "Let's see, you would have *rain* and *corn*." Ask a student to blend the parts and say the new word. (raincorn)

6. Have the puppets work together to ask the following questions. After each question have a student blend the parts and say the new word.

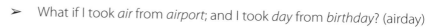

> ➤ What if I took *air* from *airport*; and I took *day* from *birthday*? (airday)

> ➤ What if I took *sun* from *sunshine*; and I took *board* from *skateboard*? (sunboard)

> ➤ What if I took *skate* from *skateboard*; and I took *bow* from *rainbow*? (skatebow)

> ➤ What if I took *wash* from *washcloth*; and I took *port* from *airport*? (washport)

> ➤ What if I took *bath* from *bathroom*; and I took *shine* from *sunshine* (bathshine)

> ➤ What if I took *pop* from *popcorn*; and I took *cloth* from *washcloth*? (popcloth)

RTI TIER LEVEL

SKILL:
Syllable Blending

MATERIALS:
Soft, squishy ball or beanbag

LITERATURE CONNECTION OPTION:
Make Way for Ducklings, by Robert McCloskey

You're One Smart Egg!

Directions:

1. Read the book *Make Way for Ducklings* to the children. Tell them that you are going to play a fun syllable game.

2. Ask each student to make a fist and pretend it is a nest. Say a word from the sample list provided, pausing briefly between each syllable. Have the students hold up one of their fingers for every syllable you say. Tell them to pretend that each finger is a duckling popping out of its egg.

3. After you've said the word in this stretched out way, ask the students to say how many parts are in the word. (Yes, they may count their fingers!) Then have them blend the syllables and say the word. Congratulate them on being such smart eggs!

4. Next, arrange the students in a circle to play Syllable-Stretch I Spy. You'll need a soft, squishy ball. Pick out something in the room that has a name with at least two syllables, such as a window. Then say, "I spy a win - dow," pausing briefly between each syllable. Throw the ball to a student who has to repeat the syllables you said and then blend them together to say the word. After the student blends the word correctly, have the student throw the ball back to you. Repeat so every child has a turn. Assist as necessary.

SAMPLE WORDS:

- duck - lings (2)
- morn - ing (2)
- mal - lard (2)
- off - i - cer (3)
- break - fast (2)
- Bos - ton (2)
- per - fect - ly (3)

- rush - ing (2)
- bi - cy - cles (3)
- head - quar - ters (3)
- po - lice - man (3)
- re - mem - ber - ing (4)

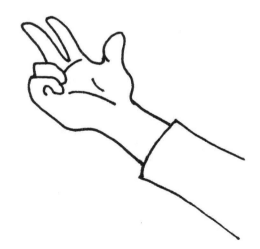

RTI TIER LEVEL

SKILL:
Syllable Blending

MATERIALS:
Puzzle reproducible on page 159

Make It Go!

Directions:

1.   Before class, copy and cut out the car and bus puzzle pieces from the reproducible on page 159. You may want to back the puzzle pieces onto card stock.

2.   Tell the student that he is going to play a word game. Demonstrate the game. Put the two car puzzle pieces on the table or desk. Leave a space between the two pieces. Tell the child that each puzzle piece stands for a syllable or a part of a word.

3.   Touch the first puzzle piece and say the first syllable in the word, pause, then touch the second puzzle piece and say the second syllable. Direct the student to touch each puzzle piece and repeat what you said. Now have the child snap the puzzle pieces together and say the word. Repeat this process using the sample words provided, or make up your own words.

4.   When the child is ready for three-syllable words, use the bus puzzle and play in the same manner as described above.

SAMPLE WORDS:

Two-syllable words:
- card - board
- can - dy
- play - ground
- book - case
- nap - kin

Three-syllable words:
- la - dy - bug
- pep - per - mint
- wood - peck - er
- thun - der - storm
- weath - er - man

RTI TIER LEVEL

SKILL:
Syllable Blending

MATERIALS:
A ball that
bounces

**LITERATURE
CONNECTION
OPTION**:
Hey, Little Ant, by
Phillip & Hannah
Hoose

Squish the Syllables

Directions:

1. Read *Hey, Little Ant*, an open-ended story about a conversation a boy is having with an ant about squishing it. Ask the student what she thinks the boy will do to the ant.

2. Tell the student that she will play a game with you about squishing syllables, not ants. Say, "Let's do a practice word from the story first. The word is *looking*."

3. Throw the ball to the student and say, "look." Have the student throw the ball back to you while saying, "ing." Now you bounce the ball once and say, "looking." Tell her that you squished the word parts or syllables together when you bounced the ball.

4. Say, "We are going to squish together words with stretched-out syllables using the bouncing ball." Tell the child that you are going to start with the stretched-out word *ti - ny*. Have her throw the ball to you while she says, "ti." Throw it back to her while you say, "ny." Then have her bounce the ball (squish the syllables) and say, "tiny."

5. Continue playing using the sample words listed below. For two-syllable words, always have the student throw the ball to you first so that on her turn she ends up blending the word. For three-syllable words, throw the ball to her first. If she is having difficulty blending the words, model a couple where you blend them. Then have her blend them.

SAMPLE WORDS:

- ba - by
- lit - tle
- squish - ing
- de - cide
- a - round
- pic - nic
- an - y - one
- fam - i - ly

RTI TIER LEVEL 1

How Many Parts Are in This Word?

SKILL:
Syllable Segmentation

MATERIALS:
Hand puppet (optional)

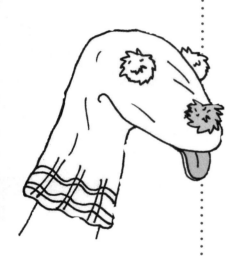

Directions:

1. If you do not have a puppet, you may want to make a simple sock puppet. Use pom-poms for the eyes and nose and a strip of red felt for the tongue.

2. Introduce the puppet, Sylvia Syllable, to your class. Tell the children that Sylvia Syllable really needs their help. She is stuck on how many parts are in some words.

3. Have Sylvia Syllable sing the following song to the children. Sing to the tune of "If You're Happy and You Know it":

   I'm stuck on how many parts are in this word.
   I'm stuck on how many parts are in this word.
   I've clapped it, and I've tapped it,
   And I've snapped it, and I've stamped it,
   But I'm stuck on how many parts are in this word.

4. At the end of the song, tell the children, "The word that Sylvia Syllable is stuck on is _____." Choose a word from the list provided, or make up one of your own. Have the children clap the word, and then call on someone to tell Sylvia Syllable how many parts or syllables are in the word. After Sylvia Syllable thanks the student, have her sing the song again. At the end of the song, give the students another word to break into syllables.

SAMPLE WORDS:

- color (2)
- funny (2)
- vacation (3)
- ball (1)
- interesting (4)
- building (2)

- animal (3)
- interrupting (4)
- computer (3)
- cafeteria (5)
- sidewalk (2)
- detective (3)

- wonderful (3)
- television (4)
- ladybug (3)
- rhinoceros (4)
- hippopotamus (5)
- helicopter (4)

SKILL:
Syllable
Segmentation

MATERIALS:
Ball of yarn

LITERATURE CONNECTION OPTION:
Spiders, by Gail Gibbons

Syllable Spiderweb

Directions:

1. Read the book *Spiders* to the children. Tell the students that they will make a spiderweb while playing a syllable game.

2. Have the class sit in a circle. Roll a ball of yarn to a student. That student is the "spider" who has to break the word you say into syllables. Tell the student to tap the ball of yarn on the floor for each syllable in the word. If the word you say is *weaving*, the student must tap the ball of yarn on the floor twice: once for the syllable *weave* and once for the syllable *ing*.

3. Ask the rest of the children to call out the number of syllables they heard after you give a silent prompt, such as holding your arm out.

4. Tell the spider to hold onto the end piece of yarn and roll the ball to another person. That person is now the spider and must break the next word you say into syllables. Use the sample words from the list provided, or make up your own.

5. Continue playing in this manner. When everyone has had a turn, the ball is finally rolled back to the original person. Now ask everyone to lift up the web and segment the word *arachnid* in a loud voice. (a - rach - nid)

SAMPLE WORDS:

- spiders (2)
- bodies (2)
- insects (2)
- spiderlings (3)
- climbing (2)
- silk (1)

- molting (2)
- web (1)
- tarantula (4)
- scary (2)
- colors (2)
- dinosaurs (3)

- animals (3)
- many (2)
- trapped (1)
- female (2)
- encloses (3)
- ballooning (3)

- climbing (2)
- molting (2)
- triangle (3)
- webbing (2)
- weavers (2)

RTI TIER LEVEL

We're Going to the Toy Store

SKILL:
Syllable
Segmentation

MATERIALS:
Reproducible
on page 160,
12 index cards,
pocket chart

Directions:

1. Before class, copy the reproducible on page 160 and cut out the pictures. These will be the "toys." Next, prepare the index cards: draw one dot on each of four index cards, two dots on another set of four index cards, and three dots on the last four index cards. The index cards will be used as pretend money.

2. Tell the children that they are going on a pretend field trip to a toy store. Show the students the toys. Go over the names of the toys with the students (they are listed in the box below). Explain that if they can tell you how many syllables are in a toy's name, they may put that toy into the group's pretend shopping cart (the pocket chart).

3. Give an example first. Hold up the picture of the football and say, "football." Clap out the word by saying the first syllable on the first clap (foot) and the second syllable on the second clap (ball). Ask, "How many syllables are in the word *football*?" (2) Have the child who gives the correct answer put the picture of the football into the pocket chart.

4. Hold up another picture. This time, have a student clap out and say how many syllables are in the word. Provide assistance as needed. The student then places the picture in the group's shopping cart.

5. Once all of the toys are displayed in the pocket chart, distribute the index card "money" to the students. Index cards with one dot can be used to "buy" toys with one-syllable names, those with two dots can be used to buy toys with two-syllable names, and those with three dots can be used to buy toys with three-syllable names.

6. Have students take turns "buying" toys from the shopping cart.

TOY NAMES:

- bat (1)
- book (1)
- doll (1)
- truck (1)
- football (2)
- baseball (2)
- puzzle (2)
- yo-yo (2)
- bicycle (3)
- butterfly (3)
- tambourine (3)
- telephone (3)

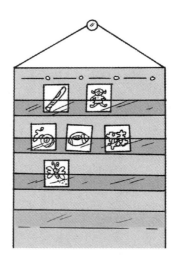

RTI TIER LEVEL

SKILL:
Syllable
Segmentation

MATERIALS:
Reproducible on
page 161,
2 square-shaped
tissue boxes,
butcher paper

**LITERATURE
CONNECTION
OPTION**:
100th Day Worries,
by Margery
Cuyler

Walking 100 Syllables

Directions:

1. Before class prepare the game board and dice. To make the game board, draw a large, circular track on the butcher paper as shown. The track must have 10 spaces. Make the spaces big enough for a student to stand in. Write the word *Start* on one space. To make the dice, copy and cut out the pictures from the reproducible on page 161. Glue one picture to each side of a square-shaped tissue box. There are 12 pictures, six for each box. (You may want to first cover the sides of the boxes in plain white paper.)

2. Read *100th Day Worries* to the children. Tell students that they are going to play a game where they work together to walk 100 syllables. Show them the game board and dice. Tell them that they are the playing pieces! Before playing, go over the names of the pictures with the students (they are listed in the box below).

3. To play, the first person rolls one die. That person says the name of the picture rolled, claps the number of syllables in that word, and walks that number of squares on the game board. For example, if the picture of the umbrella was rolled, the student would say the word *umbrella*, clap three times, and walk three squares.

4. The next player starts on the space where the first player left off (the first player sits back down). The new player rolls the other die, (alternating the die each turn will result in more word choices), says the word, claps the word, and then walks that number of spaces around the track.

5. Play until the students have collectively walked 100 spaces. To keep track of their steps, make a tally mark each time a student passes "Start."

PICTURE NAMES:

- frog (1)
- ring (1)
- apple (2)
- carrot (2)
- cookie (2)
- banana (3)

- elephant (3)
- kangaroo (3)
- popsicle (3)
- tomato (3)
- umbrella (3)
- watermelon (4)

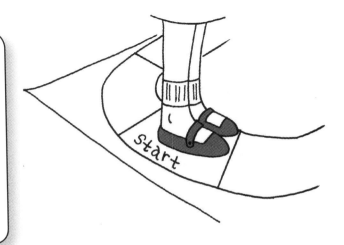

RTI TIER LEVEL

SKILL:
Syllable
Segmentation

MATERIALS:
Reproducible on
page 160,
11 x 17-inch
sheet of paper

Syllable Sort

Directions:

1. Before class, copy the reproducible on page 160 and cut out the pictures. Fold an 11 x 17-inch sheet of paper into thirds as shown to make a sorting mat. Draw one dot at the top of the first column, two dots in the second column, and three dots in the third column.

2. Tell the student that he is going to play a syllable-sorting game. Show him the sorting mat. Explain that the dots in each column stand for the number of syllables or parts in a word.

3. Before playing, go over the names of the pictures with the student (they are listed in the box below).

4. Give the child a picture card. Ask him to say the name of the picture and then clap out the number of syllables he hears in the word. If the child needs more support, instruct him to place his hand under his chin as he says the word. Tell him to count the number of times his jaw touches his hand. Once the child has successfully determined the number of syllables in the word, have him place the picture card in the correct column on the sorting mat.

5. After the student has sorted all of the picture cards, ask him to say and clap the names of all of the pictures in each column. This will give him a wonderful opportunity to hear the rhythm and cadence of one-, two-, and three-syllable words.

PICTURE NAMES:

- bat (1)
- book (1)
- doll (1)
- truck (1)
- football (2)
- baseball (2)
- puzzle (2)
- yo-yo (2)
- bicycle (3)
- butterfly (3)
- tambourine (3)
- telephone (3)

RTI TIER LEVEL

SKILL:
Syllable
Segmentation

MATERIALS:
33 sheets of
white paper

**LITERATURE
CONNECTION
OPTION**:
The Snowy Day, by
Ezra Jack Keats

Snowball Words

Directions:

1. Before class crunch up 33 sheets of white paper into balls (you may want to use sheets from the recycling bin). These will be your snowballs. Place them in a container.

2. Read *The Snowy Day* to the child. Tell the student that she is going to have fun playing with pretend snowballs. Show her the "snowballs" and tell her that she's going to use them to count syllables in the words you say.

3. Have the student stand in front of a large recycling bin. Explain that in order to play the snowball game she must take out as many "snowballs" as there are syllables in the word you say. She then gets to throw the snowballs into the bin as she says the word, one syllable at a time.

4. Demonstrate first. Say the word *snowball*. Place your pointer finger on your chin and say, "snow"; then place your middle finger on your chin next to the first one and say, "ball." Take out two wads of paper and throw them into the bin one at a time. Throw the first one in while saying *snow* and the second one in while saying *ball*. Explain that sometimes just one snowball will be used because some words only have one syllable.

5. Repeat the procedure with the sample words provided, which are from the story, or make up your own. You might want to take turns with the child and ask her to give you a thumbs-up or a thumbs-down to signal agreement with your answer. You should purposely make mistakes for the child to catch. Using non-examples is challenging for the brain. This also allows for assessing within the activity.

SAMPLE WORDS:

- looked (1)
- morning (2)
- Peter (2)
- window (2)
- street (1)
- snowsuit (2)
- outside (2)
- path (1)
- tomorrow (3)
- walking (2)
- crunch (1)
- snowman (2)
- pretended (3)
- house (1)
- wet (1)
- adventures (3)

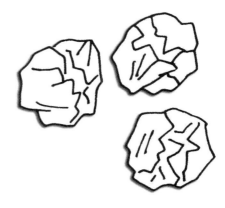

RTI TIER LEVEL 1

SKILL:
Syllable Deletion

MATERIALS:
None

Think and Pop Up!

Directions:

1. Put two chairs together, side-by-side, and ask two students to come up and sit in them. Tell the students that they are going to play a word game that involves syllables, thinking, and moving.

2. Demonstrate the game. Say the word *toothpick*. Assign one student to be the syllable *tooth* and the other student to be the syllable *pick*. Ask each student to say their syllable aloud.

3. Ask, "What is *toothpick* without *tooth*?" Give the players time to think. Tell the players that the person who has the syllable that is the answer should pop up and say her syllable. In this case, the student representing the syllable *pick* should pop up and say, "Pick." Now ask, "What is *toothpick* without *pick*?" This time the student representing the syllable *tooth* should pop up and say, "Tooth."

4. Call on two different students to come up and be the next players. Continue the activity using the sample words provided or other two-syllable words. Vary it by sometimes deleting the first syllable and sometimes deleting the second syllable.

5. As the children play, you will have the opportunity to informally assess them. If many children are struggling with these words, switch to compound words that have easily distinguishable syllables, such as the words *cupcake* and *rainbow*.

6. After every student has had a turn, you may want to set up a third chair and try the activity using three-syllable words. For example, say, "What is *understand* without *der*?" Student 1 and student 3 should pop up and each say their syllable. Ask the class to name the syllable that's left. (der)

SAMPLE WORDS:

Two-syllable words:

- mother
- sunset
- highway
- inside
- hundred
- between
- tonight
- dollhouse
- peanut
- cookie
- hammer

Three-syllable words:

- elephant
- banana
- umbrella
- antelope
- butterfly
- curious

RTI TIER LEVEL

SKILL:
Syllable Deletion

MATERIALS:
5 x 7-inch index cards, clothespins, dog puppet or stuffed animal

LITERATURE CONNECTION OPTION:
Why Do Dogs Bark?, by Joan Holub

The Syllable Dog

Directions:

1. Read several questions from *Why Do Dogs Bark?* and have the children connect the answers to their experiences with dogs they know.

2. Introduce the students to the dog puppet. Tell them that he has a strange habit. When he gets very hungry, he eats syllables. Tell the class that they will play a game. The dog will eat a part of a word, and they must try to figure out what is left.

3. Divide the class into groups of four. Give each group an index card and two clothespins. Assign a leader to each group. Tell the leaders to clip their clothespins onto the top of their cards. The clothespins will represent the syllables in the words you say.

4. Demonstrate with the word *movement*. Ask the leaders to touch the first clothespin and say, "move" and to touch the second clothespin and say, "ment."

5. Have the puppet make a munching sound and pretend that it has eaten a syllable. Say, "Oh, look! Our dog has eaten the first syllable!" Tell the leaders to take away their first clothespin. Ask a volunteer to tell you what part is left. (ment) Ask the leaders to clip the first clothespin back on and have the class say the whole word. (movement)

6. Tell the leaders to pass their cards and clothespins to another child in their group. That person is the new leader. Use the same process for the next word. Use words from the list provided, or make up your own two-syllable words. Make sure every child has a turn as the leader.

7. If the students are ready, pass out a third clothespin to each group and try the activity with three-syllable words, such as *re - triev - ers* and *an - i - mals*.

SAMPLE WORDS:

- pro - tect
- pup - pies
- bod - ies
- swim - mers
- poo - dle
- bea - gle
- lick - ing
- sniff - ing

2

RTI TIER LEVEL

SKILL:
Syllable Deletion

MATERIALS:
3 small blocks,
Velcro tape

Sticky Power, Activate!

Directions:

1. Before class, adhere Velcro to the sides of three small blocks so that they attach to each other.
   Tell the children they are Stick-On Superheroes. As Stick-On Superheroes they have the power to stick missing syllables back onto their original words. Have them practice saying, "Sticky Power, Activate!" using their best superhero voices.

2. Use the word *doghouse* to demonstrate the process. In your right hand, hold up a block and say, "dog." In your left hand, hold up a block and say, "house." Put the blocks together and say, "doghouse."

3. Now pull off the block representing the syllable house and hide it behind your back. Ask the students to say what syllable or part of the word is left. (dog) Call the Stick-on Superheroes to come to the rescue. On cue, have them shout, "Sticky Power, Activate!" Attach the block representing *house* back onto the block representing *dog*. Then invite the students to join in and say, "doghouse."

4. Continue in this manner using the sample words provided. After some practice, if your students seem ready, try this activity using three-syllable words. You will need three blocks. Ask a student volunteer to hold up the third block.

SAMPLE WORDS MODELED:

- *Jumping* is missing *ing*. What's left? (jump)
- *Pumpkin* is missing *pump*. What's left? (kin)
- *Basket* is missing *ket*. What's left? (bas)
- *Remember* is missing *re*. What's left? (mem and ber)
- *Marilyn* is missing *lyn*. What's left? (Mar and i)
- *Yesterday* is missing *ter*. What's left? (yes and day)

RTI TIER LEVEL

SKILL:
Syllable Deletion

MATERIALS:
Blue and yellow
Unifix cubes

**LITERATURE
CONNECTION
OPTION**:
*Miss Nelson Is
Missing!*, by
James Marshall

The Missing Syllables

Directions:

1. Read *Miss Nelson Is Missing!* to the students. Tell them that the children in the story were dealing with a person they thought was missing, but the children in this classroom are going to play with word parts that are missing.

2. Distribute one blue and one yellow Unifix cube to each child. Give the children a moment to put them together and take them apart.

3. Tell the children that you will say a word with two syllables. Explain that each cube will stand for one syllable. Tell students to line up their cubes on the table. Instruct them to place the blue cube first and then the yellow one. The first word is *missing*. Have all of the students point to their blue cube and say, "miss." Then have them point to their yellow cube and say, "ing."

4. Ask the students to cover up their yellow cube with their hands. Ask them what part is left. (miss) Now have them uncover the yellow cube and attach it to the blue cube and say the word *missing*.

5. Continue this process. Vary which syllable you ask the students to "hide." Sometimes they should hide the first syllable, and sometimes they should hide the second syllable. Here are some suggested words to try: d*uring, always, lessons,* and *maybe*.

6. Collect the cubes and tell the students that the following words have missing parts. Ask the students to be word detectives and tell you what part they think is left. Arrange the students in a circle. Go around the circle so each student gets a turn. Ask the following questions:

   ➤ What is *whisper* without *per*? (whis)
   ➤ What is *spitball* without *spit*? (ball)
   ➤ What is *behave* without *have*? (be)
   ➤ What is *giggle* without *gle*? (gig)
   ➤ What is *something* without *some*? (thing)
   ➤ What is *ugly* without *ly*? (ug)
   ➤ What is *homework* without *home*? (work)

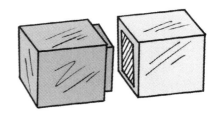

SKILL:
Syllable Deletion

MATERIALS:
Reproducible on page 162

Hide-Away Syllables

Directions:

1. Before class copy, cut out, and prepare the six flip books from the reproducible on page 162.

2. Tell the child that he will play two games. In each game, parts of words called syllables are going to hide.

3. Show the child the flip book with the pictures of the door and the bell. Have him name the pictures and figure out the compound word. (doorbell)

4. Tell the student that the syllable *bell* is going to hide. Lift up the flap with the picture of the bell. Ask the student to tell you which syllable is left. (door) Put the flap back down. Now tell the student that the syllable *door* is going to hide. Lift up the flap with the picture of the door. Ask the student to tell you which syllable is left. (bell) Continue in this manner using all of the flip books.

5. Introduce the next game. Say, "Now I'm going to hide a syllable using my hands and you'll say what is left. The first word is *picnic*."

6. Sit facing the child. Hold your right arm straight out with a fisted hand and say, "pic." Then hold your left arm straight out with a fisted hand and say, "nic."

7. Say, "I want you to say *picnic* without *nic*." Hide your left arm behind your back. Ask the student what is left. (pic)

8. Use that same method with the sample words provided or other two-syllable words. Sometimes hide the first syllable first. Sometimes hide the second syllable first. Repeat the words a second time, but this time have the child make the arm motions with you.

SAMPLE WORDS:

- winter
- super
- climbing
- jumping
- into
- mother
- healthy
- Sunday

RTI TIER LEVEL

SKILL:
Syllable Deletion

MATERIALS:
2 checkers, blue
construction
paper

**LITERATURE
CONNECTION
OPTION**:
*Oliver Button Is a
Sissy*, by Tomie
dePaola

Oliver Button Is a Word Star

Directions:

1. Before class cut out a star shape from blue construction paper. Write the words "Word Star" on it.

2. Read *Oliver Button Is a Sissy* to the student. Oliver Button practiced and practiced his talent of tap dancing, and, at the end, the kids thought he was a star and not a sissy. Tell the student that he is going to become a star, too, but his talent today involves becoming a word star.

3. Tell the student you will help him become a word star by sharing a wonderful secret for solving word riddles that uses checkers.

4. Demonstrate for the student. Say, "Here's a riddle. What would you have left if you took *old* away from *older*?"

5. Ask the student to put down two checkers next to each other. Have the student point to the first checker and say, "old." Have the student point to the second checker and say, "er." Have the child push up the checker that stands for *old* (the first one). Point to the second checker and ask the student to tell you what syllable is left. (er) Instruct the student to push the two checkers next to each before solving the next riddle.

6. Here are some word riddles to try. Add more of your own.

   ➤ What would you have left if you took *dance* away from *dancing*? (ing)
   ➤ What would you have left if you took *tures* away from *pictures*? (pic)
   ➤ What would you have left if you took *thing* away from *something*? (some)
   ➤ What would you have left if you took *be* away from *believe*? (lieve)

7. Tell the student that he now knows the secret for solving word riddles and is a word star. Congratulate him and award him the blue Word Star.

RTI TIER LEVEL

SKILL:
Phoneme Isolation of Initial Sound

MATERIALS:
Bird puppet

Hey Tweety Bird

Directions:

1. Introduce your class to Tweety Bird. (Use a bird puppet or make a stick puppet by gluing a picture of a bird onto a craft stick.) Tell the class that Tweety Bird thinks she is very smart and knows everything, but she really does need their help.

2. Read the short poem and riddle below with Tweety Bird's help:

    Teacher:
    Hey Tweety Bird, can you guess my word?
    I'll give you the first sound.

    Tweety Bird:
    Don't be absurd, I can guess any word,
    All day and all year round!

    Teacher:
    Okay. I'm thinking of a word that begins with /z/, and it is an animal with stripes. (zebra)

    Tweety Bird:
    It's a . . . uh . . . ummm . . . hmmmm . . . let's see . . .

3. When a child thinks she has the answer, have her come up and whisper the answer into Tweety Bird's ear. Have Tweety Bird whisper it into your ear. Share the student's answer with the class. Tell the children to give a thumbs-up if they think the word is correct or a thumbs-down if they disagree.

4. Repeat the poem with Tweety Bird's help using each of the riddles below:

    ➤ I'm thinking of a word that begins with /b/, and it is a fruit that has yellow skin. (banana)

    ➤ I'm thinking of a word that begins with /m/, and it is a drink that is white. (milk)

    ➤ I'm thinking of a word that begins with /l/, and it is the opposite of big. (little)

    ➤ I'm thinking of a word that begins with /r/, and it has big ears and likes carrots. (rabbit)

    ➤ I'm thinking of a word that begins with /e/, and it is a very large animal with a trunk. (elephant)

RTI TIER LEVEL

SKILL:
Phoneme Isolation of Initial Sound

MATERIALS:
None

LITERATURE CONNECTION OPTION:
The Magic School Bus At the Waterworks, by Joanna Cole

Get on the Bus

Directions:

1. Read the story *The Magic School Bus At the Waterworks* to the children.

2. Arrange chairs in rows, two-by-two, for all of the children in the class. Assign seats for the students or let them choose. Tell them that they are now on the Magic School Bus, and the person sitting next to them is their partner. Say that you are Ms. (or Mr.) Frizzle. (You might want to wear a funny hat or accessory.)

3. Tell the children that you have a fun assignment for them. They must figure out words from the story by hearing only the first sound of the word and a clue.

4. Using the examples below, give the students the first sound and clue. They may talk it over with their partner. When they think they know the answer, they should raise their hands. Call on a pair to give the answer. They may answer together.

   ➤ The first sound of the word is /b/. It's the vehicle that took the class through the water cycle. (bus)

   ➤ The first sound of the word is /w/. Two thirds of your body is made up of this. (water)

   ➤ The first sound of the word is /l/. It is a body of water. (lake)

   ➤ The first sound of the word is /r/. Water returns to Earth in the form of this. (rain)

   ➤ The first sound of the word is /m/. It's what you get when soil gets very wet. (mud)

   ➤ The first sound of the word is /f/. This takes the dirt out of water. (filter)

   ➤ The first sound of the word is /ch/. It's another name for the word *students*. (children)

5. If students need more support, add a rhyming clue. For example, say, "The first sound of the word is /b/. It's the vehicle that took the class through the water cycle, and it rhymes with *fuss*."

SKILL:
Phoneme Isolation of Initial Sound

MATERIALS:
None

You Don't Belong Here

Directions:

1. Tell the students that you are going to play a listening game.

2. To play, sing the song below to the tune of "Yankee Doodle." Then say three words. Two of the words will start with the same sound, but one will begin with a different sound (use the words from the sample sets provided). The students must listen carefully and tell you which word does not belong.

   One word has a different start sound.
   You will know it's wrong here.
   It's not hard to pick it out,
   And say, "You don't belong here."

   _____, _____, _____

3. If, for example, you said the words, *sun, top,* and *toy*, the student would answer, "Sun, you don't belong here."

4. Ask the student to explain why the word she chose does not fit. Guide the child to say something such as, "*Top* and *toy* both begin with the /t/ sound, but *sun* begins with the /s/ sound."

5. After each student has had at least two turns, go back to the first word set you used. Say, "Boys and girls, we agreed that the word *done* does not begin the same way as *rain* and *run*. What sound is at the beginning of the words *rain* and *run*?" With a partner, come up with two more words that begin with /r/." Continue in this manner using the other word sets.

SAMPLE WORD SETS:

- rain, run, done (done)
- hot, mug, hat (mug)
- boy, bat, toy (toy)
- zoo, zip, soon (soon)

- corn, top, can (top)
- man, nail, neck (man)
- pig, pat, sand (sand)
- jam, deep, jet (deep)

2

RTI TIER LEVEL

SKILL:
Phoneme Isolation of Initial Sound

MATERIALS:
Smiley-face stickers

LITERATURE CONNECTION OPTION:
The Royal Bee, by Frances Park & Ginger Park

Our Own Royal Bee

Directions:

1. Read *The Royal Bee* to the students. Tell them that Master Min taught his students many important skills so that they could learn to read and write. Tell the students that one important reading and writing skill is being able to hear and identify the beginning sounds of words. Explain that today they will practice this skill.

2. Tell the students that they are going to have their own "Royal Bee," which is different from a spelling bee. To play, you will say a word. The students must listen carefully and figure out the word's beginning sound. You might want to practice how to say letter sounds with the children as they may get confused and want to offer the letter's name.

3. Arrange the students in a circle and give each student a word for practice. (Do not use words with blends or digraphs, such as *truck* or *shirt*). Use names of things around the classroom and emphasize the first sound.

4. Once every child has had a turn to say the first sound of a word, begin again with new words. Try the sample words provided, which are from the story, or come up with your own. If a student says the letter name instead of the sound, say, "That's the letter. What's the sound?" Assist any struggling students so that at the end every student wins the Royal Bee and gets a smiley-face sticker.

SAMPLE WORDS:

- sound (/s/)
- days (/d/)
- light (/l/)
- morning (/m/)
- bell (/b/)
- master (/m/)
- read (/r/)
- soup (/s/)
- corn (/k/)
- paper (/p/)

RTI TIER LEVEL

SKILL:
Phoneme
Isolation of Initial
Sound

MATERIALS:
Paper lunch bag,
empty paper
towel tube

Going on a Sound Hunt

Directions:

1. Before class tape a paper lunch bag onto an empty paper towel tube to make a small net. (Or, if you have one, use a small fish tank net instead.)

2. Tell the child that the two of you will be going on a sound hunt. You'll both be hunting for beginning sounds. Demonstrate by saying, "I'm hunting for a sound at the beginning of a word. The sound is /d/." Then point to your desk and say, "*Desk* is a word that begins with /d/. I will put it in my net." Then pretend you are "capturing" the desk in your net.

3. Tell the child that he may think of a sound first and then find something that begins with that sound, or he may find something first and then say the sound it begins with. Demonstrate both ways for the student.

4. Give the child some time to look around the room. Then give the net to the student and watch him pretend to capture something. Ask the child to name what he captured and say its beginning sound. Then you take a turn so the child can see the task modeled. This also makes the activity more of a game, which may help motivate a struggling student.

5. Keep a list of each thing captured and who captured it. Do not let the student see the written words. Remember, phonological awareness is independent of print. When the hunt is over, read each of the things captured. Use this format:

    You captured a _____. What is the beginning sound of _____?

    I captured a _____. What is the beginning sound of _____?

6. Let the child say the beginning sound of each word.

7. If it is not practical for the student to move about the room, you might try this same activity instructing the child to cut out pictures from old magazines instead.

SKILL:
Phoneme Isolation of Initial Sound

MATERIALS:
Paper, pencil

LITERATURE CONNECTION OPTION:
The Relatives Came, by Cynthia Rylant

Finish the Shopping List

Directions:

1. Read the story *The Relatives Came*. Ask the student: Has she ever helped to grow food in a garden? What are some of her favorite foods? Does she help at the grocery store? What are her favorite items there?

2. Tell the student that you are having some relatives visit and you need to shop in the grocery store to get ready. Explain that you've been busy. You started a shopping list, but you need help to finish it. There are eight items on the list, but you were in such a hurry you only put down the first letter of each food item.

3. Tell the student that the first item starts with a /k/ sound. Say, "Which food item can it be? Is it carrots, raisins, or celery?" (carrots). Say the /k/ sound. Then say the word *carrots*. Ask if the word *carrots* begin with /k/? Say the /k/ sound again. Then say the word *raisins*. Ask if the word *raisins* begin with the /k/ sound? Do the same for the word *celery*.

4. Give the child a piece of paper numbered down from 1 to 8. Make a box on each line for the child to check. After the child correctly guesses the food item, she should put a check mark in the box—just like checking off a shopping list.

5. Here is the rest of the shopping list:

   ➤ The second item begins with the sound /m/. Is it corn, beets, or milk? (milk)

   ➤ The third item begins with the sound /l/. Is it beans, lettuce, or juice? (lettuce)

   ➤ The fourth item begins with the sound /t/. Is it tomatoes, pickles, or doughnuts? (tomatoes)

   ➤ The fifth item begins with the sound /r/. Is it yogurt, raisins, or waffles? (raisins)

   ➤ The sixth item begins with the sound /p/. Is it beef, peas, or tea? (peas)

   ➤ The seventh item begins with the sound /b/. Is it bacon, ice cream, or eggs? (bacon)

   ➤ The eighth item begins with the sound /f/. Is it macaroni, cheese, or fruit? (fruit)

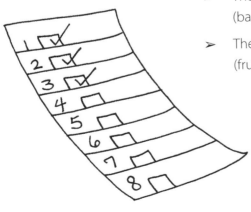

RTI TIER LEVEL 1

Can You Think of My Last Sound?

SKILL:
Phoneme Isolation of Final Sound

MATERIALS:
None

Directions:

1. Tell the children that they will be playing a listening game. To play, they must tell you the last sound of the last word they hear in your song. Sing this song to the tune of "Mary Had a Little Lamb":

   Can you think of my last sound, my last sound, my last sound?
   Can you think of my last sound?
   It's at the end of "hat".

2. Tell the children that the last word in the song is *hat*. They have to figure out the last sound in *hat*. (/t/) Sing the song again with another example. Use the word *cake*. (/k/) Once they catch on, let the students figure out the last sound for other words you place at the end of the song. Try the sample words provided, and add more of your own. If the class is ready, try the challenge words.

3. After several rounds, arrange the students in groups of four. Tell them that they have to come up with a new word for the end of the song. Have each group take a turn singing the song with their word and have the other groups tell them the ending sound.

SAMPLE WORDS:

- soap (/p/)
- fun (/n/)
- leaf (/f/)
- bill (/l/)
- rice (/s/)
- set (/t/)
- them (/m/)

Challenge words:

- fish (/sh/)
- rich (/ch/)
- ring (/ng/)
- boy (/oy/)
- sister (/er/)

RTI TIER LEVEL 1

The Important Ending Sound

SKILL:
Phoneme Isolation of Final Sound

MATERIALS:
3 noisemakers, smiley-face stickers

LITERATURE CONNECTION OPTION:
The Important Book, by Margaret Wise Brown

Directions:

1. Read *The Important Book* to the students. Tell the class that they are going to play a quiz show game called The Important Ending Sound. You will be the moderator. Have three "contestants" come up.

2. Say, "Ladies and gentlemen, welcome to The Important Ending Sound Show where I will say a word and one of the contestants will tell me the ending sound of the word. This show is unique because everybody wins. Yes, you heard me correctly! Everybody wins. Each contestant will have a turn to name the ending sound, and, get this, I can even help you out. Are you all ready to play?"

3. This first round will be a practice one. Give each contestant a practice word. Say, "Contestant number 1, what is the important ending sound in the word *rain*? Remember, do not give me the letter; give me the sound." Provide assistance as necessary. Continue in this manner, giving contestant number 2 the word *important* and contestant number 3 the word *grass*. To make it more engaging, prompt the contestants to use their noisemakers before answering the questions.

4. After a student answers correctly (even with your assistance), say, "You are correct for one smiley face. Give each contestant a sticker. Call on three new contestants to play. Use the sample words provided, or come up with your own words.

5. After each student has had a turn, try another round using the list of challenge words. Explain that because they are very tricky words (refer to page 24 to check out tricky sounds), the contestants may "use a lifeline." In other words, they may ask a classmate for help.

SAMPLE WORDS:

- smell (/l/)
- cold (/d/)
- shape (/p/)
- cheek (/k/)
- warm (/m/)
- juice (/s/)
- green (/n/)

Challenge Words:

- boy (/oy/)
- mouth (/th/)
- thing (/ng/)
- blue (/oo/)
- tender (/er/)
- ticklish (/sh/)

RTI TIER LEVEL

SKILL:
Phoneme Isolation of Final Sound

MATERIALS:
Reproducible on page 163, chalk, masking tape, beanbag

Beanbag Toss

Directions:

1. Before class, create a big tic-tac-toe board with nine squares on the floor using chalk (which vacuums up quickly) or masking tape. Copy the reproducible on page 163, and cut out the pictures. Tape one picture to the inside of each square.

2. Tell the students that they are going to play a game. They will each get a turn to toss the beanbag into one of the squares. Number off the students. Number 1 throws the beanbag first. When it lands on a picture, the student must say the name of the picture and then say the last sound heard in the word. For example, if the picture is of a cup, the student would say, "Cup, /p/." Remind students to say the *sound*, not the *letter*. Before playing, go over the names of the pictures with the students (they are listed in the box below).

3. After the player has taken his turn, ask the other students if they think he said the correct sound. Tell them to show agreement by giving the A-okay sign (thumb and pointer finger forming an O while the rest of the fingers are raised). If they disagree, tell them to form a fist.

4. Remove the picture that was just used, leaving the space blank so the remaining students will choose a new picture. Tell the next person to toss the beanbag onto another picture and repeat the process.

PICTURE NAMES:

- boat
- house
- lamp
- corn
- pail
- fork
- leaf
- nest
- pig

RTI TIER LEVEL 2

SKILL:
Phoneme Isolation of Final Sound

MATERIALS:
None

LITERATURE CONNECTION OPTION:
Check it Out! The Book About Libraries, by Gail Gibbons

Check Out My Sound

Directions:

1. Read *Check it Out! The Book About Libraries* to the students. Tell them that they are going to play a game using words from the story.

2. Line up the students so that one student is in front of another. Tell them that you are going to say a word from the story. The first person in line has to say the last sound in that word. The person behind person number 1 repeats the sound if he agrees or may challenge if he disagrees. Continue down the line. It's okay if everyone agrees, and they all say the same sound.

3. To challenge, a student must say, "I challenge you. I think the sound is _____." The two students who disagree must try to convince the other that she is correct. You be the mediator. Remember to dignify the response of each child. Say something such as, "You're right, it sounds similar to that sound", or "That's a really tricky one to hear."

4. After it goes down the line, person 1 goes to the back of the line making person 2 the new leader. Give a word to that person. The game continues until everyone has a turn to be the leader. If the interest is high, go through two rotations.

5. Before the game, give the students a practice word such as *check*. (/k/) Use the sample words from the list provided, which are from the story, or make up your own.

SAMPLE WORDS:

- big (/g/)
- small (/l/)
- books (/s/)
- public (/k/)
- collection (/n/)
- catalog (/g/)
- read (/d/)
- fine (/n/)
- budget (/t/)
- globe (/b/)

RTI TIER LEVEL

SKILL:
Phoneme Isolation of Final Sound

MATERIALS:
Big ears (purchase at a party shop) or use pictures of ears connected by pipe cleaners

What Big Ears You Have!

Directions:

1. Put on the big ears. Tell the student that she will use these big ears later to do some special listening. You are going to say three words that all end with the same sound. The child must listen carefully and figure out the sound.

2. Start with these three words: *bat, sit, feet*. Touch your big ears and say, "I hear the sound /t/ at the end of all three words." Say the three words again. Emphasize the ending sound in each word.

3. If the student agrees, tell her to give you a thumbs-up. If she disagrees, tell her to give you a thumbs-down. If the child disagrees, ask her which word did not end in the /t/ sound. Question her to determine if she is confused and thinking *beginning* sound instead of ending. Consider putting down three squares of paper, one for each phoneme of the word *bat*. Point to each square as you say each sound and then ask the child which square stands for the /t/ sound.

4. Now have the student put on the ears. Say three words that all have the same ending sound. Use words from the sample list provided, or create your own. Ask the student to say the common ending sound.

5. Some students might benefit from using a phonics phone. A phonics phone is a simple, hollow plastic tube shaped like a telephone receiver. The student speaks quietly into one end and hears her own voice through the other end.

SAMPLE WORD SETS:

- top, hope, rip (/p/)
- dog, pig, wag (/g/)
- puff, tough, knife (/f/)
- tick, back, oak (/k/)
- pal, goal, still (/l/)
- Sam, him, game (/m/)
- fib, cab, robe (/b/)
- said, red, hid (/d/)
- ten, win, bun (/n/)
- rich, patch, each (/ch/)

RTI TIER LEVEL

Sounds in the Isolation Ward

SKILL:
Phoneme Isolation of Final Sound

MATERIALS:
None

LITERATURE CONNECTION OPTION:
Germs Make Me Sick!, by Melvin Berger

Directions:

1. Read the story *Germs Make Me Sick!* to the student.

2. Tell the child that all of the words in the story came in contact with germs and had to go to the isolation ward in the Word Hospital. When they arrived at the hospital, the words were assigned to rooms based on their last sounds, just like we get assigned things based on our last names.

3. Explain, for example, that if the words *hurt, straight,* and *that* walked into the Word Hospital, the nurse in charge would assign them to the /t/ ward because all of their last sounds are /t/. Focus the student's listening by asking, "Do you hear the /t/ in *hurt*? Do you hear the /t/ in *straight*? Do you hear the /t/ in *that*?"

4. Say, "The nurse needs your help to put these words in the correct ward." Slowly say the first three words from the list of sample words provided. Model a think-aloud for the child. Show what is going on inside your head. Touch a finger to your head and pretend you are thinking. Then say, "Germ . . . /m/, some . . . /m/, them . . . /m/. I hear /m/ at the end of each word." Then say, "Words, it's the /m/ ward for you."

5. Continue in this manner. Prompt the child to think about the sound he hears at the end of each word. Then have him say, "Words, it's the _____ ward for you."

SAMPLE WORD SETS:

- germ, some, them (/m/)
- sick, make, sneak (/k/)
- throat, hot, eat (/t/)
- virus, blocks, shapes (/s/)
- sneeze, lungs, goes (/z/)
- cell, still, ball (/l/)
- blood, rid, cold (/d/)
- rash, brush, dish (/sh/)
- cuts, place, blocks (/s/)
- sleep, top, sip (/p/)
- skin, clean, medicine (/n/)
- scratch, touch, itch (/ch/)

SKILL:
Phoneme
Blending—Onset
and Rime

MATERIALS:
None

I'll Sing a Little Word

Directions:

1. Tell the class that they will play a word game. Sing this song to the tune of "Skip to my Lou":

    I'll sing a little word, and it starts with /t/.
    I'll sing a little word, and it ends with /en/.
    Put them all together, and you get "ten",
    Let's all say my word.

2. Set up three chairs in the front of the room facing the class. Ask three volunteers to come up and sit in the chairs. In front of all the children, tell person number 1 that he is the sound /t/, tell person number 2 that he is the sound chunk /en/, and tell person number 3 that she is the word *ten*.

3. Tell the volunteers that you will sing the song again. This time, when they hear their part they are to stand and stay standing. Sing the song again; invite all of the students to sing with you.

4. Thank the volunteers for helping. Tell person number 1 to go back to his seat and call on someone else to take his place. You will have a new person number 1, but the same person number 2 and person number 3.

5. In front of all the children, assign the new person number 1 the sound /p/. Tell person number 2 to keep the /en/ sound chunk, but tell person number 3 that she will have a new word. Ask the class to say the new word. (pen) Sing the song substituting the sound /p/ and the word *pen*. Have the three children stand at the appropriate times.

6. Continue that process using the following two new onsets: /m/ and /h/, making the words *men* and *hen*. Then add new onsets /b/, /p/, /t/, and /s/, and the rime /ack/, making the words *back, pack, tack,* and *sack*. Then add the onsets /p/, /b/, /w/, /f/, and /d/ and the rime /ig/, making the words *pig, big, wig, fig,* and *dig*.

RTI TIER LEVEL

SKILL:
Phoneme Blending—Onset and Rime

MATERIALS:
Chart paper, dot stickers

LITERATURE CONNECTION OPTION:
The Umbrella, by Jan Brett

The Jaguar's Spots

Directions:

1. Before class, on a piece of chart paper, draw a large oval to represent a jaguar's body, then add a circle for its head.

2. Read *The Umbrella* to the children. Remind them that, in the story, all of the animals tried to fit inside Carlos' umbrella, which was lying open on the ground in the beautiful rain forest.

3. Say to the class, "Let's pretend the animals squeezed together so hard in order to fit inside the small umbrella that they rubbed off the jaguar's spots. Class, let's help the jaguar get his spots back!"

4. Partner the students. One student is number 1 and the other student is number 2. Give each pair one dot sticker. Explain, "You and your partner have a spot to stick back on the jaguar. In order for these spots to stick on permanently, you and your partner have to figure out a word from the story that the toucan says in a funny way." Tell the students that Toucan talks by separating the first sound from the rest of the word.

5. Use the sample words provided, which are from the story, or come up with your own words. Say the word segmented into onset and rime. Call on a pair to say the whole word blended together. Every time the partners figure out a word, they get to put a spot back on the jaguar. After they put the spot on, person number 1 says the onset. Person number 2 says the rime, and the whole class says the whole word.

SAMPLE WORDS:

- much /m/ /uch/
- fig /f/ /ig/
- toucan /t/ /oucan/
- puddle /p/ /uddle/
- peep /p/ /eep/
- far /f/ /ar/
- sink /s/ /ink/

- fall /f/ /all/
- found /f/ /ound/

Challenge words:

- shake /sh/ /ake/
- start /st/ /art/
- tree /tr/ /ee/
- drip /dr/ /ip/

2

RTI TIER LEVEL

SKILL:
Phoneme
Blending—Onset
and Rime

MATERIALS:
Bubble wrap
(optional)

Snap! Crackle! Pop!

Directions:

1. Tell the students that you will say words in a funny way. First you will say just the beginning sound of a word and then stop. Then you will finish the rest of the word. Students must listen carefully and try to figure out the word.

2. Let the students know that to make the activity even more fun, they get to pop one piece of bubble wrap every time they figure out a word. (If you do not have bubble wrap the students may clap their hands instead.)

3. Demonstrate with the word *cat*. Segment it into onset and rime: /k/ /at/. Then say the whole word *cat*, while you pop one piece of bubble wrap.

4. Distribute strips of bubble wrap to the students. Tell them they may have three practice pops. If necessary, show them how to pop the bubble wrap.

5. Segment the word *cat* again. This time have the children blend the two parts together and say *cat* while they each pop one piece of bubble wrap.

6. Continue in this manner. You segment the word, and the children say the whole word while they pop one piece of bubble wrap. There will be a wonderful rhythm to it. Use the sample words provided, or add more of your own. When students are ready, include the "challenge" words.

SAMPLE WORDS:

- bone /b/ /one/
- tap /t/ /ap/
- dime /d/ /ime/
- dot /d/ /ot/
- cake /c/ /ake/

Challenge words:

- stop /st/ /op/
- blow /bl/ /ow/
- cliff /cl/ /iff/

RTI TIER LEVEL
2

SKILL:
Phoneme Blending—Onset and Rime

MATERIALS:
None

LITERATURE CONNECTION OPTION:
Stranger in the Woods: A Photographic Fantasy, by Carl R. Sams II & Jean Stoick

The Forest Animals' Surprise

Directions:

1. Read the book *Stranger in the Woods: A Photographic Fantasy* to the children. In this story, the animals discover a stranger who turns out to be a snowman built by children. The children have covered the snowman with food, such as birdseed and nuts for the animals. The animals think the snowman is a wondrous creature.

2. Tell the students that they will play a guessing game. Sing this song to the tune of "B-i-n-g-o":

   There is a snack they like to eat,
   And it begins with /n/ sound.
   /n/ /n/ /n/ /n/ /n/
   /n/ /n/ /n/ /n/ /n/
   /n/ /n/ /n/ /n/ /n/
   And it ends with /uts/.

3. At the end of the song ask the children to name the snack. (nuts)

4. Sing the song again, but this time replace the onset /n/ with /s/, and replace the rime /uts/ with /eeds/ to make the word *seeds*. Then sing it again using /k/ as the onset and /orn/ as the rime to make the word *corn*.

5. Tell the students that you'll sing a new song. Now they must figure out the name of a forest animal. Sing the following song, also to the tune of "B-i-n-g-o":

   There is a creature in the woods,
   And it begins with /m/ sound.
   /m/ /m/ /m/ /m/ /m/
   /m/ /m/ /m/ /m /m/
   /m/ /m/ /m/ /m/ /m/
   And it ends with /ouse/.

6. After singing the song, ask the children to name the forest animal. (mouse)

7. Continue in this manner, changing the onset and rime to name these creatures: *doe*, *rabbit*, *fawn*, and *bird*.

SKILL:
Phoneme Blending—Onset and Rime

MATERIALS:
Reproducible on page 157, 6 elastic bands

Stretch It Out

Directions:

1. Before class, make a copy of the reproducible on page 157. Cut out one picture box. Cut that picture in half (make a vertical cut), and then fold each cut piece in half by bringing the top edge down to the bottom edge as shown.

2. Cut two small slits about a quarter of an inch apart on the fold of each piece. Open up the pieces and thread an elastic band that has been cut once to form a straight line through the slits. Thread both halves of the picture onto the same elastic band. Arrange the pieces side-by-side so you can see the whole picture. Repeat this procedure with the remaining pictures and elastic bands.

3. Tell the student that he will play a game. You will say a word in a stretched-out manner, and he will have to guess the word. Say /d/ /og/ while stretching out the elastic band with the dog picture pieces. (It helps to hold the side of each picture when stretching out the elastic band.) Now relax the elastic band so the two halves form a whole picture of a dog and ask the student to say the word in the normal way. (dog)

4. Continue in this manner using the other pictures you have prepared. The picture cards include: pot /p/ /ot/, soap /s/ /oap/, coat /k/ /oat/, fish /f/ /ish/, key /k/ /ey/, and dog /d/ /og/.

5. For additional practice, give the student a cut elastic band. Tell him to listen carefully and stretch out the elastic band while you say a word in a stretched out manner (use the sample words provided, or come up with your own). Then instruct him to relax the elastic band and say the word blended together. The student will not have the support of the pictures, but he will have the use of a hands-on manipulative.

SAMPLE WORDS:

- face /f/ /ace/
- nest /n/ /est/
- pet /p/ /et/
- tail /t/ /ail/
- hop /h/ /op/
- car /k/ /ar/

RTI TIER LEVEL

I See a /B/ /ear/ Looking at Me

SKILL:
Phoneme Blending—Onset and Rime

MATERIALS:
Big fake glasses

LITERATURE CONNECTION OPTION:
Brown Bear, Brown Bear, What Do You See?, by Bill Martin Jr.

Directions:

1. Read *Brown Bear, Brown Bear, What Do You See?* to the student.

2. Tell the student that she is going to play a game. You will say a poem that is similar to the one used in the story, but you will say the name of each animal in a special way. The child's job is to figure out the name of the animal that you "see." Give the student the big glasses to put on (or make binoculars by taping together two empty toilet tissue rolls). Recite this poem:

   Sarah, Sarah (replace with the name of your student)
   What do I see?
   I see a /b/ /ear/ looking at me.

3. If necessary, guide the child to notice that you separated the word *bear* by saying the first sound and then the rest of the word. Ask the child to say the name of the animal with the sounds blended together.

4. Read the poem several more times. Each time, replace the word *bear* with another animal from the list provided, or add your own animal words.

SAMPLE WORDS:

- cat /k/ /at/
- horse /h/ /orse/
- shark /sh/ /ark/
- dog /d/ /og/
- worm /w/ /orm/
- goat /g/ /oat/
- rat /r/ /at/
- skunk /sk/ /unk/

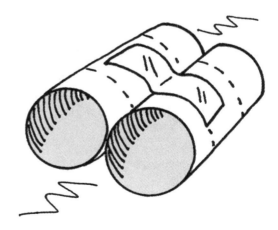

SKILL:
Phoneme Blending—All Phonemes

MATERIALS:
Notepad and pen

A Diner Called /E/ /T/

Directions:

1. Tell the students that they are going on an "in-house" field trip to a diner that is very popular. Everybody wants to go there. It is so popular that you need reservations to get a table. Tell them that you made a reservation six months ago for the whole class and today is the big day!

2. The name of the diner is /E/ /t/. Each sound is said separately. That is what is so unique about this diner. The waiters and waitresses tell you the different foods they offer by segmenting every sound. The customers have to figure out the foods. Everyone loves eating at /E/ /t/ because it is so much fun to guess what's on the menu.

3. Line up the students at the door of your classroom. Pretend they are entering the diner. Say, "Welcome to the /E/ /t/ Diner where the names of our foods are stretched out. This way to your table please." Escort the students to their normal classroom seats, but pretend that it is the diner.

4. Hold your notepad and pen and pretend to be a waitress. Tell the children the food choices by segmenting the name of each food. Read the names of the foods from the sample word list provided, or make up your own foods. As the students guess what each item is, pretend to take their orders and say phrases that a waitress in a diner might use such as "excellent choice" and "coming right up!"

SAMPLE WORDS:

- soup /s/ /oo/ /p/
- meat /m/ /e/ /t/
- chicken /ch/ /i/ /k/ /e/ /n/
- peas /p/ /e/ /z/
- steak /s/ /t/ /a/ /k/
- eggs /e/ /g/ /z/
- mac & cheese /m/ /a/ /k/ and /ch/ /e/ /z/

- doughnut /d/ /o/ /n/ /u/ /t/
- milk /m/ /i/ /l/ /k/

Challenge words:

- fish sticks /f/ /i/ /sh/ /s/ /t/ /i/ /k/ /s/
- hot dogs /h/ /o/ /t/ /d/ /o/ /g/ /z/
- French fries /f/ /r/ /e/ /n/ /ch/ /f/ /r/ /i/ /z/
- ice cream /i/ /s/ /c/ /r/ /e/ /m/

RTI TIER LEVEL 1

SKILL:
Phoneme Blending—All Phonemes

MATERIALS:
None

LITERACY CONNECTION OPTION:
WBUG Radio Up Close and Personal: An Interview with Harry the Tarantula, by Leigh Ann Tyson

The Nervous Interview

Directions:

1. Read *An Interview with Harry the Tarantula* to the children. Katy Did interviewed Harry the Tarantula and learned all about tarantulas. If you don't have the book, talk about what an interview is. Perhaps have a student interview you.

2. Explain to the students that sometimes guests on radio or TV shows are a little nervous while being interviewed. Tell the students to pretend that Harry was very nervous. He was so nervous that he couldn't say all his words correctly, and Katy Did had a hard time understanding him. Invite the students to help Harry.

3. Divide the class into groups of four and have the children in each group count off so that there is a number 1, 2, 3, and 4 in each group. (It's okay if a group has one fewer or one more. If there is one more, then that group would have two students with the number 1.) Tell the groups that you are going to say a word in the broken up way that Harry said the word. They have to discuss with each other and determine what they think the word is.

4. Call out a number from 1 to 4, or use a spinner. Let's say you called out the number 2. All of the number 2s would stand up. Say a word by slowly segmenting each sound in the word. If the word is *legs*, for example, you would say /l/ /e/ /g/ /z/. Give the students time to confer with their teams then call on one student to tell the class what her group thinks Harry's word is. Have the class show agreement with a thumbs-up or thumbs-down signal.

5. Continue by calling out a number and segmenting a word sound-by-sound. Use the words provided, which are from the story, or make up your own words. Every group should have at least two turns to answer.

SAMPLE WORDS:

*   legs /l/ /e/ /g/ /z/
*   mice /m/ /i/ /s/
*   shed /sh/ /e/ /d/
*   lump /l/ /u/ /m/ /p/
*   hillside /h/ /i/ /l/ /s/ /i/ /d/
*   female /f/ /e/ /m/ /a/ /l/

*   fangs /f/ /a/ /ng/ /z/
*   climb /k/ /l/ /i/ /m/
*   host /h/ /o/ /s/ /t/
*   true /t/ /r/ /oo/
*   stars /s/ /t/ /ar/ /z/
*   skunks /s/ /k/ /u/ /n/ /k/ /s/

RTI TIER LEVEL

Smart Slinky and Slide a Sound

SKILL:
Phoneme Blending—All Phonemes

MATERIALS:
Little slinkies, one for each student (optional)

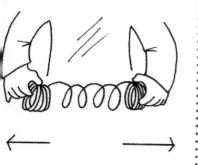

Directions:

1. Tell the students that they are going to exercise their brains and their muscles with two activities.

2. The first activity is called Smart Slinky. Demonstrate for the group how to stretch the word *pen* sound by sound, using a slinky. As you say each sound, /p/ /e/ /n/, stretch the slinky a little farther apart. Then ask the students to say the word blended together. As they say the word, you push your slinky back together.

3. Give each student a slinky. If you don't have slinkies, tell them to use their pretend slinkies (this really does work well—students just go through the stretching motions).

4. Tell the students to stretch their slinkies out little by little as they listen to each sound you say. (You should stretch your slinky out, too.) When you are finished saying all of the sounds, ask everybody to push their slinkies back together and say the whole word.

5. After you do several rounds with the entire group calling out the word at the end, do a few more, but this time call on a volunteer to say the word. Use the three- and four-phoneme words from the sample list provided.

6. The next activity is called Slide a Sound. Teach the children how to blend three-phoneme words using their arms. With your right hand, touch your left shoulder and say /p/. Move your hand down to your elbow, stop there and say /i/. Move your arm down to your wrist, stop there and say /g/. Now bring your right hand back up to your shoulder and slide down your whole arm saying the word *pig*. Have the students practice this method using the word *pig* again. Continue in this manner using the three-phoneme sample words provided.

SAMPLE WORDS:

Three-phoneme words:
- can /c/ /a/ /n/
- bone /b/ /o/ /n/
- hat /h/ /a/ /t/
- wake /w/ /a/ /k/
- chin /ch/ /i/ /n/
- name /n/ /a/ /m/
- net /n/ /e/ /t/
- sock /s/ /o/ /k/

Four-phoneme words:
- sand /s/ /a/ /n/ /d/
- lamp /l/ /a/ /m/ /p/
- flag /f/ /l/ /a/ /g/
- flip /f/ /l/ /i/ /p/

SKILL:
Phoneme
Blending—All
Phonemes

MATERIALS:
1 pipe cleaner
and 5 plastic
beads per
student

**LITERACY
CONNECTION
OPTION**: *The
Memory String*, by
Eve Bunting

Sound String

Directions:

1. Read *The Memory String* to the students. Tell the students that you are going to show them a different kind of memory string called a sound string. The beads on your string will represent the sounds in words.

2. In front of the students, string three beads onto a pipe cleaner (you may want to bend the ends to prevent the beads from sliding off).

3. Tell the students that you are going to segment, or stretch out, some of the words in the story using your sound string. Say the word *Jane*, one sound at a time: /J/ /a/ /n/. As you say each sound, slide one bead to the middle of your pipe cleaner. Leave a little space between each bead. Next, push the beads together and say the word *Jane* blended together.

4. Pass out one pipe cleaner and three beads to each student. Give them a moment to string their beads. Have the students push their beads close to their right hand. Ask the students to repeat each sound you say while they push one bead to the left. Instruct them to leave a small space between each bead. After saying each sound in the word, the students should push their beads together and tell you what the word is. Try the following three-phoneme words:

   /d/ /a/ /d/ (dad), /o/ /l/ /d/ (old), /l/ /e/ /f/ (leaf), /c/ /a/ /t/ (cat)

5. Give the students each another bead to add to their pipe cleaners. Repeat the process above using the following four-phoneme words:

   /h/ /e/ /l/ /p/ (help), /d/ /r/ /e/ /s/ (dress), /s/ /t/ /o/ /p/ (stop)

6. Tell the children that you are going to give them two extra-hard words. They are going to have to really listen and think, but you believe they can do it. Have them each add a fifth bead to their pipe cleaners. Stretch out the following five-phoneme words:

   /b/ /u/ /t/ /o/ /n/ (button), /s/ /t/ /r/ /i/ /ng/ (string)

7. For struggling students, go back to the three-phoneme words. Use counters or manipulatives to scaffold, or break the words into onset and rime.

RTI TIER LEVEL

SKILL:
Phoneme
Blending—All
Phonemes

MATERIALS:
Puppet with
movable mouth

Story Helper

Directions:

1. If you do not have a puppet to use, make a simple puppet using a paper lunch bag decorated with markers.

2. Introduce the student to your puppet friend Caitlin. Say that Caitlin wants to tell a story, but sometimes she has trouble saying whole words. What she ends up doing is stretching out the sounds of the word. Tell the child that he can be the "story helper" and help Caitlin by telling her the words with all of the sounds blended together.

3. Say, "Let me tell you how she will stretch out the words so you will be prepared to be the best story helper ever!" Segment the word *dog* (/d/ /o/ /g/), and then ask the student to say it blended together. If the student struggles, ask him to hold up one finger per sound as you say each sound. Then move your finger across the child's three fingers as if to blend the word as the child says, "dog."

4. If the child still struggles, divide the word into onset and rime (/d/ /og/) and see if that works. If it does, go back to segmenting each sound (/d/ /o/ /g/). If that doesn't work, segment a two-phoneme word from the story below such as *it* (/i/ /t/). Then build up to three-phoneme words that start with a continuant sound, such as in the word *mom* (/m/ /o/ /m/). (See Tips for Sounding Out Letters on pages 20–21.)

5. When the child is ready, tell the following story while holding the puppet. Each time you see a segmented word, have the puppet stretch it out and ask the child to blend the sounds and say the word. Then continue with the rest of the story.

Mike woke up one morning very excited. He and his /d/ /o/ /g/, Casey, were going to go to his Cousin Valerie's birthday party across town. For the first /t/ /i/ /m/, he was going to take a bus alone, if you don't count Casey. He practiced taking the /b/ /u/ /s/ with his older brother last week, and now he was ready to go on his own. He could hardly /e/ /t/ his breakfast he was so excited. He kept asking his mom, "Is it time yet? Is it time yet?" His /m/ /o/ /m/ kept answering, "Soon." After what seemed like forever, Mom finally said it was time to /g/ /o/. He took his bus money, Valerie's birthday present, and Casey and went off to ride a bus alone for the first time. It was going to be the /b/ /e/ /s/ /t/ day ever!

RTI TIER LEVEL

SKILL:
Phoneme
Blending—All
Phonemes

MATERIALS:
4 Unifix
cubes, purple
construction
paper, yarn

**LITERATURE
CONNECTION
OPTION**:
*Lilly's Purple Plastic
Purse*, by Kevin
Henkes

Connect-A-Word

Directions:

1. Before class fold a piece of purple construction paper into thirds to make the shape of a purse. Secure each side with tape. Punch holes in the top corners of the purse. Thread yarn through the holes and tie the ends for a handle. Put four Unifix cubes in the purse.

2. Read *Lilly's Purple Plastic Purse* to the student. Talk about why Lilly's teacher, Mr. Slinger, took away her purse. Ask the student to recall what was in the purse when Mr. Slinger gave it back to Lilly.

3. Show the student the purse. Take out three of the Unifix cubes and put them in front of you. Explain that you will stretch out a word sound by sound, and the student will use the Unifix cubes to connect the sounds and figure out the word.

4. Model the process. Put three Unifix cubes in front of you in a row. Say, "I will say a three-sound word from the story. As I say each sound, I will touch a cube." Touch the first cube as you say /l/, the second cube as you say /o/, and the third cube as you say /t/. Sweep your finger under the cubes and say, "lot." Now repeat each sound as you connect the Unifix cubes. Say the word *lot* again.

5. Separate the cubes and give them to the student. Say, "We are going to do a practice run. Put the three cubes in a row. I will slowly say each sound in the word. Touch one cube for each sound you hear. Listen carefully, /l/ /o/ /t/. Now, connect the cubes and say the whole word." If the student is having difficulty blending, scaffold by stretching the word several times, progressing from very slow to normal speed.

6. Repeat the activity with the following three-phoneme words. After each word, have the student separate the cubes.

   /p/ /ur/ /s/ (purse), /t/ /oo/ /n/ (tune), /l/ /a/ /b/ (lab), /b/ /e/ /l/ (bell)

7. Try these four-phoneme words. The student will need the fourth cube still inside the purse. These are challenge words. Remember to scaffold if necessary by stretching the words several times, progressing from very slow to normal speed.

   /s/ /k/ /oo/ /l/ (school), /d/ /e/ /s/ /k/ (desk), /s/ /n/ /a/ /k/ (snack)

RTI TIER LEVEL 1

SKILL:
Phoneme Segmentation

MATERIALS:
Puppet and toy hammer

We Are Construction Workers

Directions:

1. Tell the children that they are all going to pretend they are construction workers. Introduce the class to the puppet, Chuck, who is their boss or foreman. Have Chuck hold a toy hammer. (If you do not have a puppet to use, cut out a picture of a construction worker and glue it to a craft stick. Make a hammer from card stock and attach it to the puppet's arm.)

2. Have Chuck say, "Okay, boys and girls, your job today is to break apart words. It's going to be a tough job." Have Chuck demonstrate. "Here's how it works. I'll tell you a word. The word I am going to demonstrate is *bed*. Watch what I do." Have Chuck "bang" the hammer down three times. Each time he bangs the hammer down he says a sound. First /b/, then /e/, and then /d/. Have Chuck say, "Okay, any questions?"

3. Next, have Chuck say, "Your teacher is going to distribute pretend hammers to each one of you. You will use these hammers to break apart words. Remember, safety first. Do not use the hammers for any other purpose!" Pantomime distributing hammers.

4. Have Chuck say a word. Use the sample word list provided, or make up your own words. In unison, the class segments the word into its individual sounds, making one bang per sound. In order for the children to make a banging sound, show them how to hold one hand open flat while they use the other hand (made into a fist) to strike their open palm. After the class works together to segment a word, have Chuck call on a volunteer to segment the same word again independently.

SAMPLE WORDS:

- mop /m/ /o/ /p/
- get /g/ /e/ /t/
- step /s/ /t/ /e/ /p/
- cake /k/ /a/ /k/
- ten /t/ /e/ /n/
- lunch /l/ /u/ /n/ /ch/

- bye /b/ /i/
- guest /g/ /e/ /s/ /t/
- paper /p/ /a/ /p/ /er/
- house /h/ /ou/ /s/
- fox /f/ /o/ /k/ /s/

Unflatten Flat Stanley

SKILL:
Phoneme
Segmentation

MATERIALS:
Unflatten
Flat Stanley
reproducible
on page 165,
newspaper

**LITERATURE
CONNECTION
OPTION**:
Flat Stanley, by Jeff
Brown

Directions:

1. Before class, make three copies of the Flat Stanley reproducible on page 165. Cut out two of the pictures and staple them together, leaving a small opening on one side. Wad up small pieces of newspaper and stuff them into the opening. When Flat Stanley looks full, staple the opening shut. Cut out the third copy of Flat Stanley and keep it flat.

2. Read the story *Flat Stanley*. Talk about some of the things Flat Stanley was able to do because he was flat. Say, "It was lucky that Stanley's brother, Arthur, was able to unflatten Stanley, but if his idea didn't work I've thought of another one that might." Tell the children that your idea is to whisper words in a stretched out way into Flat Stanley's ear. You think that might make Flat Stanley stretch back to his normal size, too.

3. Show students the cut-out of Stanley that is flat. Say, "I'll call on someone to whisper a word into Flat Stanley's ear in a stretched out way. I'll do the first one to show you how. The word is *bed*." Segment the word *bed* by saying the sounds /b/ /e/ /d/ into Flat Stanley's ear.

4. Use the words from the list provided, or make up your own. Call on students to come up and segment words into Flat Stanley's ear. After the last word, switch the cut-outs of Flat Stanley from the flat one to the filled-out one. Try to make the switch without the children noticing. Tell the students that it looks like they were able to unflatten Flat Stanley. "See, stretching out the words did work! Hooray for you!"

SAMPLE WORDS:

- kites /k/ /i/ /t/ /s/
- string /s/ /t/ /r/ /i/ /ng/
- shouts /sh/ /ou/ /t/ /s/
- sneak /s/ /n/ /e/ /k/
- plan /p/ /l/ /a/ /n/
- had /h/ /a/ /d/
- flat /f/ /l/ /a/ /t/
- pocket /p/ /o/ /k/ /e/ t/

- search /s/ /er/ /ch/
- notice /n/ /o/ /t/ /i/ /s/
- empty /e/ /m/ /p/ /t/ /e/
- attached /a/ /t/ /a/ /ch/ /t/

Challenge words:
- painting /p/ /a/ /n/ /t/ /i/ /ng/
- Stanley /s/ /t/ /a/ /n/ /l/ /e/

SKILL:
Phoneme
Segmentation

MATERIALS:
None

Body Talk

Directions:

1. Tell the students that you will teach them how to figure out how many sounds, or phonemes, are in a word by using their bodies. Tell them that you will start with two-sound words and then move up to more challenging three- and four-sound words.

2. Have them watch as you demonstrate a two-phoneme word. Start with the word *it*. Touch your chin with your pointer finger and say /i/ (keep your other fingers folded inward). Pull your pointer finger slightly away from your face, then retouch your chin adding in your tall-man finger, and say /t/. Now count the fingers that you used. Ask the students to say how many sounds are in the word *it* while you hold up your two fingers.

3. Ask the students to stand up and use their fingers to segment words with two-phonemes or sounds. Try the following words: *at, in, Ed, me, of, on,* and *up*.

4. Tell the students that they will now use their bodies to count words with three-phonemes. Demonstrate with the word *cat*. Touch your head and say /c/. Touch your waist and say /a/. Touch your toes and say /t/. Then say, "cat."

5. Give the students practice segmenting words with three-phonemes. Remind them to use their heads, waists, and toes. Some words to try include *can, hat, red, sip,* and *dot*.

6. Prepare students to try something even harder—four-phoneme words that start with a consonant blend, such as the word *stop*. Touch your head and say /s/. Touch your shoulders and say /t/. Touch your waist and say /o/. Touch your toes and say /p/. Some words for the students to try include *flag, clap, step, frog,* and *slip*.

7. When the students are ready, teach them to segment five-phoneme words with beginning and ending consonant blends, such as the word *trust*. Demonstrate how by touching your head, shoulders, waist, knees, and toes as you segment each sound. Some words for the students to try include *blast, clasp, crisp,* and *crust*.

RTI TIER LEVEL

SKILL:
Phoneme
Segmentation

MATERIALS:
Reproducible
on page 164,
counters

**LITERATURE
CONNECTION
OPTION**:
Freight Train, by
Donald Crews

Conductor School

Directions:

1. Before class make one copy of the reproducible with the Elkonin boxes on page 164 for each student. For this activity, the students will need only the Elkonin box with four squares, so you may want to cover or cut off the Elkonin box with three squares.

2. Read *Freight Train* to the children. Ask if they have ever seen a freight train or been on a real train. Tell the children that today they will go to conductor's training school to learn how to load freight on a special sound train.

3. Distribute the Elkonin boxes and four counters to each student. Say, "Welcome to conductor training school. Today you will learn how to load freight. This train carries three- and four-sound words. Your job is to put one sound from each word into its own car. The counters represent the sounds, and the boxes on your papers stand for the train cars."

4. Model the activity. Place your counters under the boxes—one counter per box. Say, "The word is *ride*." Say /r/ and slide the first counter into the first box; say /i/ and slide the second counter into the next box; say /d/ and slide the third counter into the third box. (If a child asks about the letter e at the end of *ride*, acknowledge that there is an e at the end of the word, but today you are working on sounds, not letters.) Explain that some words will just have three sounds so a box will be left over, and some words will need all four boxes. Ask the students to practice loading their "freight cars" using the word *ride*.

5. Choose a student to be the lead conductor. Say a word from the sample list provided, or make up your own words. Ask the lead conductor to say each sound in the word while the other students (including the conductor) slide one counter into each box for every sound. Give each student at least two turns as the lead conductor.

SAMPLE WORDS:

- fast /f/ /a/ /s/ /t/
- cab /c/ /a/ /b/
- bell /b/ /e/ /l/
- track t/ /r/ /a/ /k/
- chug /ch/ /u/ /g/

- train /t/ /r/ /a/ /n/
- cap /c/ /a/ /p/
- steam /s/ /t/ /e/ /m/
- coal /c/ /o/ /l/

RTI TIER LEVEL

SKILL:
Phoneme Segmentation

MATERIALS:
Reproducible on page 158, two 5 x 8-inch index cards

PICTURE NAMES:

- cup
- dime
- hand
- cake
- flag
- mop
- plane
- sock
- tent

Pop-Up Sound Sort

Directions:

1. Before class, copy and cut out the pictures from the reproducible on page 158.

2. Use the instructions below to make two pop-up cards, one with three boxes and one with four boxes:

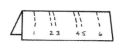

- *Fold the top edge of the index card down to the bottom edge, "hot dog" style. Press to crease.*

- *Cut six 1-inch parallel slits on the creased edge. Allow for 1¼-inches between slits 1 and 2, 3 and 4, and 5 and 6. Allow for ½-inch between slits 2 and 3 and 4 and 5 as shown.*

- *Fold the 1-inch cuts toward the open edge and press to crease.*

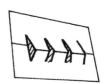

- *Open the card and push the 1-inch creased boxes into the inside opening. Close the card and press flat.*

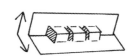

- *Open the card and the boxes will pop up.*

- *To make a pop-up card with four boxes, follow the steps above, but cut five slits.*

3. Show the student the picture cards and both pop-up cards. Explain to the student that she will use the pop-up cards to figure out how many sounds are in the words featured on the picture cards.

4. Demonstrate with the picture of the cup. Use the three-phoneme pop-up card (the one with the three boxes). Touch each pop-up box as you say the sounds in the word *cup*. (/k/ /u/ /p/) Now use the four-phoneme pop-up card and segment the word *cup* again. Point out that since there is an extra box, this picture belongs under the card with three pop-up boxes. Ask the child to place the picture of the cup under the card with the three pop-ups.

5. Give the student another picture card. Ask her to say the name of the word on the card sound-by-sound using the three-phoneme pop-up card. Each time she says a sound, she should touch one box. Ask, "Were there enough boxes for every sound?" If so, tell her to place the picture under the card; if not, have her try the four-phoneme pop-up card. Assist as necessary.

RTI TIER LEVEL

Monster Talk and Monster Walk

Directions:

SKILL:
Phoneme Segmentation

MATERIALS:
4 carpet squares, green construction paper, craft stick

LITERATURE CONNECTION OPTION:
The Teacher from the Black Lagoon, by Mike Thaler

1. Before class, cut out a monster shape from green construction paper (or use a picture of a monster), and glue the monster onto a craft stick.

2. Read *The Teacher from the Black Lagoon*. In the story, the little boy falls asleep in class and dreams that his new teacher, Mrs. Green, is really a green monster. He imagines that she'll eat the children or turn them into frogs! Of course, when he wakes up, he meets his teacher and discovers she is very nice.

3. Tell the student that you once knew a teacher named Mrs. Green. Say, "Of course she wasn't a real monster either, but she did teach her class monster talk!" Explain that "monster talk" is when you stretch a word out into each of its sounds and use a big, deep voice. Demonstrate monster talk for the word *bag*. (Say each sound using a big, deep, monster voice, /b/ /a/ /g/.)

4. Tell the child that you will say a word and he has to repeat it using monster talk. Give him the monster on the stick to help. He should tap the monster on the table or desk once for each sound he says. Use the sample words provided, or make up your own words.

5. Your kinesthetic learners will especially enjoy the next part of this activity. Put down four carpet squares to create a path (or tape four pieces of construction paper to the floor). Tell the student that now he will walk like a monster, too. Demonstrate "monster walk" by walking with your legs straight and both arms extended out in front of you. Using the sample words again, ask the student to segment each word using monster talk and simultaneously monster walk as he moves one square per sound.

SAMPLE WORDS:

- sit /s/ /i/ /t/
- be /b/ /e/
- desk /d/ /e/ /s/ /k/
- name /n/ /a/ /m/
- lip /l/ /i/ /p/
- pile /p/ /i/ /l/
- just /j/ /u/ /s/ /t/

RTI TIER LEVEL

SKILL:
Phoneme
Deletion of Initial
Sound

MATERIALS:
None

Guess a Name

Directions:

1. Tell the students that they are going to play a guessing game with partners.

2. Explain that you are going to say a student's name without its first sound. The partners must talk and decide whose name you are saying. When you call on a pair, one partner says the person's name and the other partner says the sound that was left off. (Naming the sound that was deleted and the word part that remains are important components of this skill, so be sure to have students practice both.)

3. Use each student's name in the game. Watch out for tricky ones. For example, a name that begins with a consonant blend such as *Stan* would be *Tan*. A name that begins with a vowel such as *Ellen* would be *Len*. A name that begins with a digraph such as *Chad* would be *Ad*.

4. Next, tell the partners to put their heads together and come up with two words. Tell them to practice saying the words without their beginning sounds.

5. Now pair up the partners to make groups of four. If you have an uneven number of students, it's okay to create groups of three or five. Tell the two pairs to face each other. The pair closest to the door goes first and says its first word without the first sound. The other pair tries to figure out the word and say the missing first sound.

6. Then the pairs switch, and the other set of partners shares one of its words without its first sound. The pair that is now guessing tries to figure out the word and say the missing first sound.

7. Pairs continue taking turns in this way until both pairs have shared both of their words.

SKILL:
Phoneme Deletion of Initial Sound

MATERIALS:
Notebook

LITERATURE CONNECTION OPTION:
A Picture Book of Anne Frank, by David Adler

Dear Diary

Directions:

1. Read *A Picture Book of Anne Frank*. Talk about how difficult it was for everyone to hide for so long. Explain that Anne passed the time by writing in a diary.

2. Tell the children that diaries usually contain private thoughts. Show the students a notebook and say that it is your diary. Tell them that you wrote a letter to the class in your diary. Explain that you didn't want just anyone to read your private thoughts so you wrote some of the words using a secret code. After they play this game, they should be able to figure out the words in your letter.

3. Tell them that your secret code was to leave off the first sound in a word. Acknowledge that guessing words without beginning sounds can be tricky, but this warm-up activity will help them. Read the following riddles to the class:

   ➤ What's missing in *ear* that you hear in *dear*? (/d/)

   ➤ What's missing in *lass* that you hear in *class*? (/k/)

   ➤ What's missing in *tudents* that you hear in *students*? (/s/)

   ➤ What's missing in *ery* that you hear in *very*? (/v/)

   ➤ What's missing in *ames* that you hear in *games*? (/g/)

   ➤ What's missing in *rick* that you hear in *trick*? (/t/)

   ➤ What's missing in *ucky* that you hear in *lucky*? (/l/)

4. Now that the students have practiced naming missing sounds in words, read the following letter with the missing sounds. Call on students who think they can figure out the words.

> *_ear _lass,*
>
> *I love having you for my _tudents. You are good listeners, you work well together, and you are all _ery smart. One of my favorite activities to do with you is play word _ames. It is hard for me to _rick you because you are all so good with words. I am _ucky to have a class with all of you in it.*
>
> *Love,*

RTI TIER LEVEL 2

SKILL:
Phoneme Deletion of Initial Sound

MATERIALS:
Reproducible on page 158, 9 counters per student

Sound Off!

Directions:

1. Before class make a copy of the reproducible on page 158 for each student. These will be the game cards.

2. Tell the children that they will play a game called Sound Off. Distribute nine counters and a game card to each student. Go over the names of each picture (the picture names are listed below).

3. Ask the students to say the name of each picture without its first sound. For example, *cup* without its first sound would be *up*.

4. Say, "Here's how to play. Look at the pictures on your card. I am going to say the name of one picture with its beginning sound taken off. You try to figure out which picture it is. If you think you know, call out 'Sound Off!' Do not say the name of the picture, just put a counter on it. There are no winners or losers in this game."

5. Say, "Find a picture of an *ent*." Allow students time to figure out the word and put a counter over the picture of the tent. Then call on a student to say the sound that was left off of the word. (/t/)

6. Continue in this manner, calling out the following word endings: /up/, /ime/, /and/, /ake/, /lag/, /op/, /lane/, and /ock/.

7. After the game, pair the students and have them practice saying the words on their game cards without their first sounds. For example, person 1 would say, "*Cup* without /k/ is *up*." Then person 2 would say, "*Dime* without /d/ is *ime*."

PICTURE NAMES:

- cup
- dime
- hand
- cake
- flag
- mop
- plane
- sock
- tent

RTI TIER LEVEL

SKILL:
Phoneme Deletion of Initial Sound

MATERIALS:
None

LITERATURE CONNECTION OPTION:
Stellaluna, by Janell Cannon

Bat Children

Directions:

1. Read *Stellaluna* to the children. Remind the children that bats like to sleep hanging upside down. Tell the children to pretend they are bats and (carefully) lean over their tables or desks with their heads hanging down.

2. Tell them that you are going to ask them some easy questions. You won't ask hard ones because it's hard to think upside down when you're not a bat. Explain that you will ask questions about some of the sounds that begin words used in the story.

3. Say the word *night* by elongating the /n/ sound. (n-n-n-n-ight) Then say *ight*. Ask the children if they can figure out what sound has been taken away. The answer is /n/. Tell the students to sit upright in their chairs and take a deep breath so they can think.

4. Give each student a question using the same process. Elongate the first sound in each word and then say the word without the first sound. Use the sample questions provided, or add some of your own.

5. Tell them that since they did such a good job with those words, you are going to ask some harder questions. They have to figure out a word without its beginning sound. Form the questions in this format:

   ➤ *Fall* without its first sound is _____. (all)

   ➤ *Wings* without its first sound is _____. (ings)

   ➤ *Flap* without its first sound is _____. (lap)

   ➤ *Green* without its first sound is _____. (reen)

SAMPLE QUESTIONS:

- S-s-s-stellaluna, tellaluna. What is the first sound that I took off? (/s/)
- F-f-f-food, ood. What is the first sound that I took off? (/f/)
- M-m-m-mother, other. What is the first sound that I took off? (/m/)
- B-b-b-birds, irds. What is the first sound that I took off? (/b/)
- D-d-d-day, ay. What is the first sound that I took off? (/d/)
- N-n-n-nest, est. What is the first sound that I took off? (/n/)

SKILL:
Phoneme
Deletion of Initial
Sound

MATERIALS:
Green and red
construction
paper

Abracadabra

Directions:

1. Before class, cut one 3 x 3-inch square from green construction paper and four 3 x 3-inch squares from red construction paper.

2. Tell the student that she will be playing a word game called Abracadabra. In this game you magically change a word into a new word by taking away its first sound!

3. Place one green square and two red squares in a row on the table or desk. Tell the student that each square represents a sound. Use the word *sit* as an example. Point to each square and say the sound it represents. (/s/ /i/ /t/) Now sweep your finger under the squares and say the word *sit*.

4. For added support, place two more red squares underneath the first set. Tell the student that these squares represent the same sounds /i/ and /t/. Sweep your finger underneath the squares and say the word *it*. Ask the student, "What sound is missing from the word *sit* to make the word *it*?" Guide her to point to the first green square in the top row and say /s/.

5. Model once more using the word *tan*. Place the green square and the two red squares on the table. Guide the student to point to each square and say each sound. (/t/ /a/ /n/) Have the student sweep her finger under the squares and say, "tan." Tell the student to remove the square that stands for the /t/. Ask what word is left. The student should say, "Abracadabra, the new word is *an*." Hold the student's finger under the red squares and sweep it from left to right saying the word *an*. Ask the student again what word she made. (an) Then ask the student what sound she took away to make the new magic word. (/t/)

6. Use the sample words provided. You'll notice that they have four letters, but three sounds.

SAMPLE WORDS MODELED:

word	word segmented	remove	new word
cake	/k/ /a/ /k/	/k/	ache
seat	/s/ /e/ /t/	/s/	eat
hill	/h/ /i/ /l/	/h/	ill
goat	/g/ /o/ /t/	/g/	oat
cash	/c/ /a/ /sh/	/k/	ash
mice	/m/ /i/ /s/	/m/	ice

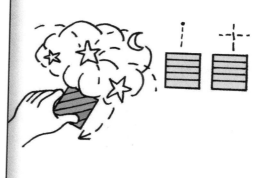

RTI TIER LEVEL

SKILL:
Phoneme
Deletion of Initial
Sound

MATERIALS:
None

**LITERATURE
CONNECTION
OPTION**:
The Kissing Hand,
by Audrey Penn

Helping Hands

Directions:

1. Read *The Kissing Hand*. Remind the child about the secret Chester's mother told him. She kissed his hand and said that whenever he felt lonely at school he should press his hand to his cheek and he'd feel the warmth of her love.

2. Tell the student that today you will share a special secret for using hands to help figure out word riddles.

3. Use the word *kiss* as an example. Ask the child to hold out both hands palms up. Touch the student's left palm and say /k/. Gently help the child fold his hand to "hold" that sound. Next touch the student's right palm and say, "/iss/." Again, gently fold the student's hand to hold that sound chunk. Touch the student's left hand and say, "/k/"; then touch his right hand and say "/iss/." Point to the student's left hand and ask, "What sound is in there?" (/k/) Point to the student's right hand and ask, "What sound chunk is in there?" (/iss/)

4. Now ask the student, "What would *kiss* be without /k/?" Instruct the child to put his left hand behind his back and then to open his right hand and say the word chunk he is "holding." (/iss/)

5. Continue in this manner using the sample questions provided.

SAMPLE QUESTIONS:

- What would *hand* be without /h/? (and)
- What would *heart* be without /h/? (eart)
- What would *home* be without /h/? (ome)
- What would *rush* be without /r/? (ush)
- What would *may* be without /m/? (ay)
- What would *told* be without /t/? (old)
- What would *nights* be without /n/? (ights)
- What would *feel* be without /f/? (eel)
- What would *toys* be without /t/? (oys)

Challenge questions:

- What would *swing* be without /s/? (wing)
- What would *play* be without /p/? (lay)

RTI TIER LEVEL 1

SKILL:
Phoneme Deletion of Final Sound

MATERIALS:
2 noisemakers or bells

The Make New Words Show

Directions:

1. Tell the students that they are going to play a quiz show game called The Make New Words Show. The object of the game is to make a brand-new word by taking off the final sound in a word. Give an example. Say, "What sound do I have to take off the word *meat* to make the word *me*?" (/t/)

2. Partner the children; they are the contestants. If there is an uneven number, it's okay to have a group of three people.

3. You are the game show host. Say, "Welcome to The Make New Words Show where we take off final sounds of words and make brand-new words. First, let's meet our contestants." Call up a pair. You may want to briefly interview the contestants by asking them to say their names and a favorite number, color, or flavor of ice cream.

4. Say, "All right contestants, let's get started. Good luck to you. Our first question is, 'What sound do I have to take off the word *make* to make the word *may*?'" Give the partners time to consult with one another; tell them to use their noisemakers to let you know when they have the answer.

5. Congratulate partners when they answer correctly and assist them when they need help. There are no losers. Everybody wins. Call up the next pair to play. Continue until each pair has had at least one turn.

6. Here are the questions:

    ➤ What do I have to take off the word *plant* to make *plan*? /t/

    ➤ What do I have to take off the word *farm* to make *far*? /m/

    ➤ What do I have to take off the word *note* to make *no*? /t/

    ➤ What do I have to take off the word *pile* to make *pie*? /l/

    ➤ What do I have to take off the word *time* to make *tie*? /m/

    ➤ What do I have to take off the word *start* to make *star*? /t/

    ➤ What do I have to take off the word *need* to make *knee*? /d/

    ➤ What do I have to take off the word *great* to make *grey*? /t/

    ➤ What do I have to take off the word *teeth* to make *tea*? /th/

    ➤ What do I have to take off the word *weed* to make *we*? /d/

    ➤ What do I have to take off the word *bust* to make *bus*? /t/

    ➤ What do I have to take off the word *nose* to make *no*? /z/

RTI TIER LEVEL 1

SKILL:
Phoneme Deletion of Final Sound

MATERIALS:
None

LITERATURE CONNECTION OPTION:
So Many Circles, So Many Squares, by Tana Hoban

Circle Partners

Directions:

1. Look at the wordless book *So Many Circles, So Many Squares* with the children. Take a few minutes to let the children talk about circle and square shapes they see in the classroom.

2. Tell the students that you are going to teach them a sound game. For the game, they will use their bodies to form circles.

3. Divide the class into two groups. Have the children stand in their groups. Instruct one group to form a circle facing in and the other group to form an inside circle facing out. The class will have formed two circles, one on the inside and one on the outside, with each person facing a partner.

4. Tell the class that you will say a word. The students must first repeat your word, and then work with their partners using "whispering voices" to figure out the last sound in the word. For example, if you say the word *hand,* the whole class repeats "hand" in unison, and then the partners quietly figure out the last sound, /d/.

5. Tell the students that once they think they have figured out the last sound, they should sit down in the circle. When all pairs are seated, call on one pair to share the answer. If they are correct, all students stand back up for the next word. If their answer is not correct, call on another pair.

6. Continue in this manner using the sample words provided, or make up your own.

SAMPLE WORDS:

- make
- rich
- silly
- bell
- coat
- great
- girls
- teacher
- best
- mother
- mouse
- cup
- book
- phone
- window
- desk

RTI TIER LEVEL

Grab Bags

Directions:

SKILL:
Phoneme Deletion of Final Sound

MATERIALS:
4 paper lunch bags, various classroom objects

1. Before class prepare four grab bags. To prepare each one, fill a paper lunch bag with at least four objects (or pictures of objects) whose names all end with the same sound. For example, one bag could include a book, a stick, a fork, and a rock, since those words all end with the sound /k/. Another bag could include a pencil, a marble, a shell, and a ball, since those words all end with the sound /l/. See the list of sample objects for more ideas.

2. To begin, let the students see you empty the contents of one bag onto the table. Ask the students to name each object. Challenge them to figure out the ending sound that all of the objects have in common.

3. Once they have figured out the common sound, give each student one of the objects and ask each one to say the name of the object without its last sound. For example, if a child is holding a fork, he would say *for*.

4. Continue in this manner using each of the bags you have prepared.

5. Next, empty the contents of all of the bags onto the table and mix them up. Ask the children to work together to sort them back into the correct bags based on their last sounds.

SAMPLE OBJECTS:

objects ending with /k/	objects ending with /er/	objects ending with /l/	objects ending with /n/
book	marker	marble	pen
block	ruler	tile	chain
chalk	paper	ball	stone
stick	eraser	bell	balloon
clock	flower	doll	fan
cork	hammer	wheel	pan
fork	feather	apple	can
rock	quarter	pail	
sock	spinner	label	
toothpick			

RTI TIER LEVEL

SKILL:
Phoneme
Deletion of Final
Sound

MATERIALS:
Reproducible on
page 164, scissors
for each child

**LITERATURE
CONNECTION
OPTION**:
*Franny B. Kranny,
There's a Bird in
Your Hair!*, by
Harriet Lerner &
Susan Goldhor

Sound Cuts

Directions:

1. Before class, make four copies of the reproducible with the Elkonin boxes on page 164 for each student, plus one for yourself. Cut out the Elkonin boxes so that each child will have four Elkonin boxes with three squares and four Elkonin boxes with four squares.

2. Read the story *Franny B. Kranny* to the students. Franny had long, frizzy hair and did not want to cut it. A bird actually built a nest in it!

3. Tell the children about a peaceful town called Soundsville where words live. Unlike Franny, the words like to go to the barber. Once a month all of the words go to the sound barber for a final-sound cut. When they get out of the barber's chair, they all feel like new words. For example, when "bead" goes in to get his sound cut, he comes out "bee." The sound barber always cuts off the final sound.

4. Tell the children that you will teach them how to be barbers just like the one in Soundsville. Pass out one Elkonin box with three squares and a pair of scissors to each student. Guide the students through the practice word *and*. Have them point to each square on the Elkonin box while they say the sounds in the word. (/a/ /n/ /d/) Tell them to cut off the last sound. Ask the students to say what final sound they cut off (/d/). Now have them say the new word (an).

5. Continue in this manner using the words from the list provided, or make up your own three- and four-phoneme words. Give each child a turn to say the final sound that was cut off and the new word.

SAMPLE WORDS MODELED:

word	word segmented	remove	new word
made	/m/ /a/ /d/	/d/	may
seat	/s/ /e/ /t/	/t/	see
team	/t/ /e/ /m/	/m/	tea
tent	/t/ /e/ /n/ /t/	/t/	ten
party	/p/ /ar/ /t/ /e/	/e/	part
mend	/m/ /e/ /n/ /d/	/d/	men

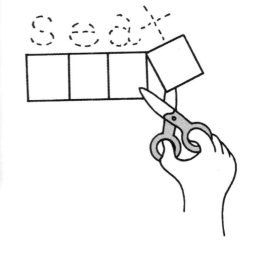

RTI TIER LEVEL

SKILL:
Phoneme Deletion of Final Sound

MATERIALS:
Unifix cubes, game board with path, game piece

Snap and Go

Directions:

1. Tell the student that she is going to play a word game. Explain that to play, you will take the last sound off a word to make a new word. If the child can figure out the new word, she may move forward one space on the game board. Use an existing game board that has a path or make one by drawing spaces on a piece of paper.

2. Show the student three Unifix cubes that are snapped together. Explain that each cube will represent one sound in a word that you will say. Use the word *team* as an example. Point to the first cube and say, "/t/." Then point to the second cube and say, "/e/." Then point to the last cube and say, "/m/." Run your finger under all three and say, "team." Snap off the last cube and say, "I'm removing the /m/ from *team*. What word is left?" If the child guesses correctly (tea) she may move one space on the game board.

3. If the child doesn't know the answer, try scaffolding using the process above, but use two Unifix cubes. Say a two-phoneme word, such as *in*. Ask the student to name the *sound* that is left instead of the *word* that is left.

4. Give the student the three attached Unifix cubes. Say a word. Have the child touch each cube and say each sound in the word. Next ask the student to run her finger under the cubes and say the word. Finally, have the child remove the last cube and ask what is left. Review by asking, "What sound did you take away from (the original word) to make (the new word)?" Have the student move up a space on the game board.

5. Use words from the list provided, or make up your own words. Give the student an extra Unifix cube for the four-phoneme words.

SAMPLE WORDS MODELED:

word	word segmented	remove	new word
bake	/b/ /a/ /k/	/k/	bay
bean	/b/ /e/ /n/	/n/	bee
time	/t/ /i/ /m/	/m/	tie
paid	/p/ /a/ /d/	/d/	pay
pant	/p/ /a/ /n/ /t/	/t/	pan
grape	/g/ /r/ /a/ /p/	/p/	gray

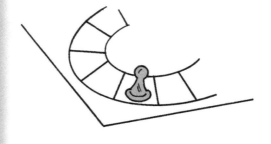

RTI TIER LEVEL

SKILL:
Phoneme
Deletion of Final
Sound

MATERIALS:
Shark picture,
craft stick, 4
checkers

**LITERATURE
CONNECTION
OPTION**:
Sharks, by Gail
Gibbons

The Hungry Sound Shark

Directions:

1. Make a shark puppet by gluing a picture of a shark onto a craft stick.
2. Read *Sharks* to the student. Review the different kinds of sharks mentioned in the book. Tell the student that you have brought in another shark not mentioned in the story. Introduce her to Sound Shark. Hold up the shark puppet and have it say this poem:

   I'm a hungry sound shark.
   Sounds are what I eat.
   The ending sounds in all the words
   Are such a tasty treat!

3. Put out three checkers in a row. Say, "This row of checkers is for the word *bone*." Point to each checker as you say the sounds in the word *bone*, /b/ /o/ /n/. Then sweep your finger under the checkers and say, "bone."
4. Have the shark recite the poem again, but this time, make the shark "eat" the /n/ sound by sliding away the last checker. Ask the student what remains of the word. Sweep your finger under the remaining two checkers and help her say, "/bo/."
5. Continue in this manner using the sample words provided. Allow the student to use the shark puppet to make the shark "eat" the final sound in each word. After the student removes the sound, ask her to say the new word. Tell the student that sometimes the word that is left will be a real word and sometimes it will be a silly word.

SAMPLE WORDS MODELED:

word	word segmented	remove	new word
shark	/sh/ /ar/ /k/	/k/	shar
guide	/g/ /i/ /d/	/d/	guy
fish	/f/ /i/ /sh/	/sh/	fi
teeth	/t/ /e/ /th/	/th/	tea
made	/m/ /a/ /d/	/d/	may
fins	/f/ /i/ /n/ /z/	/z/	fin
meat	/m/ /e/ /t/	/t/	me

RTI TIER LEVEL 1

SKILL:
Adding Phonemes

MATERIALS:
None

Ta Da!

Directions:

1. Tell the class that they are going to play a word game called Ta Da. Explain that a magician says, "Ta Da!" when he does something magical. The game is called Ta Da! because the students will be doing something magical—making new words appear!

2. Ask the children to count off by threes. Assign the 1s the /s/ sound, the 2s the /f/ sound, and the 3s the /k/ sound.

3. Say, "To play the game, I will call out a word and a number. If I call your number, you must add your sound to the beginning of my word to make a new word. Once you figure out the new word say, 'Ta Da!'"

4. Give this example. "Let's say I called out the word *ink* and the number one. Those of you who are number 1s have the /s/ sound. If you add /s/ to *ink*, the new word is *sink*. If you are a number 1 and you figure out that the new word is *sink*, stand up and say, 'Ta Da!' Then I'll call on one person to say the new word."

5. Continue playing in this manner using the sample words provided.

SAMPLE WORDS:

For the /s/ sound:
- it (sit)
- end (send)
- and (sand)
- at (sat)

Challenge words:
- pin (spin)
- top (stop)

For the /f/ sound:
- an (fan)
- or (for)
- in (fin)
- ace (face)

Challenge words:
- lap (flap)
- runt (front)

For the /k/ sound:
- all (call)
- ape (cape)
- it (kit)
- oat (coat)

Challenge words:
- rib (crib)
- lap (clap)

RTI TIER LEVEL
1

SKILL:
Adding
Phonemes

MATERIALS:
1 ball per group
of students, music

**LITERATURE
CONNECTION
OPTION**:
Chrysanthemum,
by Kevin Henkes

The Wondrous Ball

Directions:

1. Read *Chrysanthemum* to the children. It's a story about a girl who is teased by her classmates. Ask students to indicate by a show of hands if they have ever been teased. Respond by saying something such as, "That is no fun. In this class, Chrysanthemum would feel welcome because we celebrate each other."

2. Tell the class that they are going to play a word game to practice appreciating each other. Divide the class into groups of about six. Have each group form a circle. Select one student in each group to be the "starter."

3. Explain the game. Say, "I will say a word ending, such as /op/, and I will assign the ball a sound, such as /m/. When I start the music, each starter is to say the sound and then pass the ball to the person on his right. That person repeats the sound and then passes the ball to the next person. You will continue passing the ball around the circle until the music stops. Whoever has the ball when the music stops is "it." That person has to blend the /m/ sound with /op/ and say the word *mop*, but only when I give the signal."

4. Give the starter in each group a ball. Assign a beginning sound and select a word ending (see the sample word list for suggestions). After you stop the music, give the students about 30 seconds of "think time" before signaling the children who ended up with the ball to shout out the word.

5. Tell the remaining group members to celebrate their classmates' success by giving them applause or words of encouragement, such as "Right on!" or "Good job!" or "You are so-o-o smart!"

SAMPLE WORDS MODELED:

word ending	beginning sound	new word
other	/m/	mother
ake	/k/	cake
est	/b/	best
inner	/d/	dinner
etals	/p/	petals
Challenge words:		
anted	/ch/	chanted
ink	/th/	think
cool	/s/	school

RTI TIER LEVEL

SKILL:
Adding
Phonemes

MATERIALS:
Construction
paper, 2
beanbags, basket

Sillytown Fair

Directions:

1. Before class make raffle tickets by cutting construction paper into 1 x 2-inch rectangles. Make several tickets for each student.

2. Read the children this story:

    There was a town called Sillytown. Its mayor was a sweet little old lady named Mayor Schnizeldorfer. She loved her town. Everybody there had silly names and loved to say silly words and laugh. One day she decided to have a fair with a parade and games. Her favorite person, Silly Sound Clown, was going to be in charge of the town's favorite game booth, playing everyone's favorite game, the Silly Word Game.

3. Announce to the group that it's their lucky day. They will get to play the Silly Word Game! You'll teach them how. Put a beanbag on the table. Say, "This beanbag stands for the word ending /am/." Place another beanbag in front of the first one and say, "This beanbag stands for the sound /f/." Model how to blend them together. "Fff-am, fff-am, fam. The silly word is *fam.*" Model several more times. Use a different word chunk and beginning sound each time. Once the students seem ready, say "Let's go to the fair!"

4. Start the game. You play the Silly Sound Clown. (You might want to wear a silly hat.) Hand out several tickets to each child. Throw a beanbag into the basket and say, "itch." Choose a player. Ask the player for a ticket. Give him a beanbag. Assign the beanbag the sound /z/. The player says the silly word, *zitch,* and throws the beanbag into the basket. That player chooses a new player. If a player gets stuck, the other students can help. Use words from the list provided, or make up your own words.

5. If students struggle, choose easier word chunks, such as *an, in, ed, at, op,* and *up.*

SAMPLE WORDS MODELED:

word chunk	beginning sound	silly word
unk	/k/	kunk
orgle	/d/	dorgle
off	/j/	joff
oomer	/f/	foomer

RTI TIER LEVEL 2

Surgery at the Word Hospital

SKILL:
Adding Phonemes

MATERIALS:
3 red tiles, 1 yellow tile, small tray

LITERATURE CONNECTION OPTION:
The Magic School Bus Inside the Human Body, by Joanna Cole

Directions:

1. Read *The Magic School Bus Inside the Human Body*. Ms. Frizzle, the teacher, could magically take students inside the body and study its parts.

2. Say, "Let's pretend to visit the word hospital. I'll be Dr. Goodword, the surgeon, and you'll be my assistants. Let's pretend to scrub up and put on our surgical masks and gloves. (You may want to put on some real ones.) We're going to perform surgery by attaching new sounds onto word parts."

3. Demonstrate with the word *us*. Place two red tiles on the table. Choose an assistant to hold the tray with the yellow tile on it. Point to each tile on the table and say the sound of each phoneme, /u/ /s/. Then run your fingers under the two sounds and say, "us."

4. Ask your assistant to take the tile from the tray and put it down in front of your tiles. Tell the group that the new tile stands for the sound /b/, and your assistant has attached it to the word *us*. Ask everyone to say, "/b/." Now ask them to say, "us." Ask, "Who thinks they can say the new word?" After a student answers, run your finger under the three tiles and say, "bus." Remove the tiles.

5. Each time you perform a new "surgery," choose a new assistant. Follow the same process using the sample words provided, or make up your own words. Place down two red tiles for the two-phoneme words and three red tiles for the three-phoneme words. The student will always place down the yellow tile.

SAMPLE WORDS MODELED:

word ending	beginning sound	new word
/er/ /m/	/g/	germ
/ar/ /t/	/h/	heart
/r/ /a/ /n/	/b/	brain
/o/ /d/ /e/	/b/	body
/u/ /ng/	/l/	lung
/p/ /i/ /n/	/s/	spine

RTI TIER LEVEL

Amaze Your Friends!

SKILL:
Adding
Phonemes

MATERIALS:
Pocket chart,
red and green
construction
paper

Directions:

1. Before class cut two squares from construction paper that will fit into your pocket chart. Make one green and the other red.

2. Tell the student that you are going to play a game where silly words are turned into real words. Tell the student each time she turns a silly word into a real one, the two of you, just for fun, get to wiggle your fingers and say, "Amaze your friends!"

3. Put up a pocket chart for the child to see. Leave the first pocket in the first row of the pocket chart empty. Put a red square in the second pocket. Tell the child that the red square represents the silly word *op*. Ask the child to say, "op."

4. Hold up a green square and say, "This square represents the sound /m/." Have the child say, "/m/." Ask the child to put the /m/ square in the empty pocket in front of the red square representing the sound /op/. Invite the child to blend it together with you, "mmm-op, mop!" Run your finger underneath the squares as you blend the word *mop*. Give the child a turn to do it, too. Now you and the student wiggle your fingers and say, "Amaze your friends!"

5. Continue that process, but from this point on, have the child try to figure out the word by blending it independently. If the child struggles, hold the child's finger under the squares representing the sounds and slowly blend the word. Then do it again and blend it a little faster. Finally, say the word all blended together. Use the list of sample word endings and beginning sounds, or come up with your own. The possibilities are endless!

SAMPLE WORDS MODELED:

word ending	beginning sound	new word
ent	/s/	sent
oy	/b/	boy
ap	/l/	lap
est	/n/	nest
unny	/f/	funny
ack	/t/	tack
een	/s/	seen

RTI TIER LEVEL

SKILL:
Adding
Phonemes

MATERIALS:
Two small stuffed
animals, sheet of
paper

**LITERATURE
CONNECTION
OPTION**:
Ira Sleeps Over, by
Bernard Waber

Silly Word or Real Word?

Directions:

1. Read *Ira Sleeps Over* to the student. In the story, Ira has a dilemma. Should he take his teddy bear to his friend's house? Ask the student if he ever had a teddy bear or favorite stuffed animal. If so, ask its name.

2. Tell the child that you'll teach him a fun game he can play at a sleepover. Show the student your stuffed animals and say, "We're going to use Farfel and Moppet to help us play. Can you tell me what sound Farfel begins with? (/f/) How about Moppet? (/m/) In this game we will be adding those sounds to make words. Which sound do you want to be?" Let the student decide if he wants to be /f/ or /m/. You be the other sound. Let's say the child chooses the /f/ sound.

3. Make a scoreboard by drawing three columns on a sheet of paper. Put the child's name on the top of the first column, your name on the top of the next one, and write "silly words" on the top of the last column.

4. Say, "Here's how we play. Let's use the word ending /at/. You can go first. Blend your sound /f/ onto /at/. What is the word? (fat) Is that a real word? Yes! You score a point. Now it's my turn. I'm going to blend /m/ onto /at/. What's my word? (mat) Is that a real word? Yes! I score a point, too. No points for the silly-word column."

5. Continue in this manner using the sample word endings below, or make up your own word endings. If the child is having difficulty, let him use chips to represent the sounds. Ask the child to touch each chip as he says the sounds. Then have the child sweep his hand under the chips and blend the parts together.

SAMPLE WORD ENDINGS:

- eet
- ox
- ant
- ake
- all

- un
- it
- in
- ist

1

RTI TIER LEVEL

SKILL:
Phoneme
Substitution of
Initial Sound

MATERIALS:
Reproducible on
page 163

Turn Man Into Pan

Directions:

1. In advance, cut out the pictures from the reproducible on page 163. You will need all of the pictures except for the pictures of the lamp and the pail.

2. Tell the students that they will play a word game. Divide the class into groups of four. (It's okay if groups have one more or fewer.) Assign each group a leader. Pass out one picture to each group (depending on how many students you have, a few pictures may be leftover). Go over the name of the picture with each group (they are listed in the box).

3. Put three chairs in front of the class. Invite three children to come up. (Do not invite a student who is a leader to come up yet.) Say, "My three helpers are going to help me make a word." Point to the top of the first person's head and say, "/m/." Point to the top of the second person's head and say, "/a/." Point to the top of the third person's head and say, "/n/." Slide your hand above the heads of all three as you say the word *man*.

4. Ask the students to work together in their groups to decide if they have the picture with the beginning sound that would change *man* into *pan*. The leader from the group with the picture of the pig should come up and exchange places with the person sitting in the first chair. The students representing the sounds /a/ and /n/ are to remain seated. Ask someone in the "pig" group to explain how *man* turned into *pan*.

5. Continue in this manner instructing the class to make the words *can* (the leader with the picture of the corn replaces the first person) and *fan* (the leader with the fork picture replaces the first person). After each word change, ask the students to explain how the word changed into the new word.

6. Invite three new students to come up and assign those students the sounds for the word *sit*. Now challenge the groups to make the words *bit, hit, kit, fit, lit,* and *pit*.

PICTURE NAMES:

- boat
- house
- corn
- fork
- leaf
- nest
- pig

SKILL:
Phoneme
Substitution of
Initial Sound

MATERIALS:
None

**LITERATURE
CONNECTION
OPTION**:
Fly Away Home,
by Eve Bunting

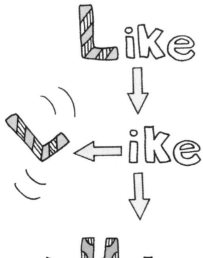

Homeless Words

Directions:

1. Read the book *Fly Away Home* to the class. Talk about how hard the homeless father and son worked at not getting caught while living in the airport.

2. Say to the class, "Let's pretend there were some homeless words living in the airport, too. They worked hard at not getting caught, and they came up with a plan. Each day they changed how they looked and that way nobody recognized them. The way they did that was to change their first sound every day. For example, the word *home* changed its first sound to /k/ and became *comb*. No one would ever realize that *comb* was once *home*. Aren't the words clever?"

3. Divide the class into four groups. Have each group stand in one of the four corners of the classroom. Explain that you are going to give each group a word and a sound. The group must figure out what the word becomes without its first sound and what the word becomes with the new sound. Assign each group its word and sound. No group may start discussing until all four groups have their words and sounds.

4. Give the groups some time to discuss. Choose a number from one to four, and call on that group. Ask a volunteer to share her group's original word, the word without its first sound, and the new word. After all four corners have shared, give each group a new word plus sound and repeat the procedure. Use the examples provided below:

   ➤ *Caught* changed its first sound from /k/ to /b/. What did it become? (bought)

   ➤ *Get* changed its first sound from /g/ to /p/. What did it become? (pet)

   ➤ *We* changed its first sound from /w/ to /s/. What did it become? (see)

   ➤ *Ten* changed its first sound from /t/ to /h/. What did it become? (hen)

   ➤ *Change* changed its first sound from /ch/ to /r/. What did it become? (range)

   ➤ *Blue* changed its first sound from /b/ to /f/. What did it become? (flew)

   ➤ *Cart* changed its first sound from /k/ to /d/. What did it become? (dart)

   ➤ *Like* changed its first sound from /l/ to /h/. What did it become? (hike)

2

RTI TIER LEVEL

SKILL:
Phoneme Substitution of Initial Sound

MATERIALS:
10 small paper plates, 10 craft sticks

Food Lollipops

Directions:

1. Before class cut out 10 food pictures from magazines or grocery store circulars. Each food item should have a different beginning sound. Glue one picture to the front of each paper plate. Tape a craft stick to the back of each paper plate. You now have 10 food "lollipops."

2. Show the children the lollipops. Ask them to say the name and first sound of each of the foods pictured. Tell the group that you will use the food lollipops to play a game.

3. Demonstrate the activity. Give one student a food lollipop. The student holds the lollipop by the stick. The picture should face the other students. The student must name the food and say the word's first sound. For example, if the lollipop had a picture of chili on it, the student would say, "This is chili and its first sound is /ch/."

4. Call on another student to stand beside the student holding the chili lollipop. Let's say the student's name is Mason. Sing this song to the tune of "If You're Happy and You Know It":

   If you take away the /m/ in Mason's name
   If you take away the /m/ in Mason's name
   If you take away the /m/ and replace it with a /ch/
   Can you tell us how you'll say this brand new name?

5. The person holding the food lollipop must think and say, "Chason." If the student needs more support, ask Mason to say his name without the /m/. (Ason) Then have the person holding the picture add the /ch/ sound. (Chason) Ask the rest of the group, "What did the student holding the lollipop have to do to change *Mason* to *Chason*?"

6. Tell the students to go back to their seats. Put the chili food lollipop away and take out another one with a different food. Call on two new helpers and follow the same procedure.

RTI TIER LEVEL

SKILL:
Phoneme Substitution of Initial Sound

MATERIALS:
Small snack foods (such as cereal or raisins)

LITERATURE CONNECTION OPTION:
Diary of a Worm, by Doreen Cronin

Worm Ate His Homework

Directions:

1. Read *Diary of a Worm* to the students. Through the hilarious pictures and funny anecdotes in worm's diary, children learn all about the ups and downs of being a worm through a worm's eyes. One day the worm actually ate his homework!

2. Tell the children that today they get to pretend to be worms, but they get to eat real treats!

3. Say, "Imagine that you are a worm. Your teacher asked you to bring in worm-related words for an important assignment. You did a great job, but, on the way to school, you did what you always do; you ate your homework. You didn't mean to do it. You tried hard not to do it. In fact, you ate only the first sound of each word. You hoped you could replace the sounds when you got to school. But when you got there, you couldn't remember what they were so you replaced them with different sounds. Let's act out the story."

4. Ask for a volunteer to be your "worm." Put two raisins in a row so that the group can see them. Tell the children you chose the word *dig* for your homework. Touch the first raisin and say, "This raisin stands for the /d/ in *dig*." Touch the second raisin and say, "This raisin stands for the rest of the word /ig/." Sweep your finger below each raisin and say, "dig." Now say, "The worm is so hungry that it's going to eat the /d/." (Have the volunteer eat the first raisin.) "Uh, oh! What's left?" (Have the volunteer say /ig/.) "I'll need to replace the first sound, but I can't remember what it is. Oh, well, I guess I'll just use a /p/." Put a new raisin in front. Ask the volunteer to say the new word. (pig)

5. Choose a new volunteer and continue in this manner using the words listed below. Assist as necessary. Give each student at least two turns.

   ➤ Replace the /w/ in *wiggle* with /g/. What do you get? (giggle)

   ➤ Replace the /m/ in *mud* with /b/. What do you get? (bud)

   ➤ Replace the /w/ in *worm* with /t/. What do you get? (term)

   ➤ Replace the /s/ in *soil* with /b/. What do you get? (boil)

   ➤ Replace the /b/ in *bait* with /w/. What do you get? (wait)

   ➤ Replace the /d/ in *dirt* with /sh/. What do you get? (shirt)

RTI TIER LEVEL

SKILL:
Phoneme Substitution of Initial Sound

MATERIALS:
Tiles of 2 different colors

Doodledeedoo, Sound Switcharoo

Directions:

1. Tell the student that you are going to show him a fun trick. By replacing the first sound in a word with another sound, you will make a brand-new word. Put three tiles of one color in front of you so that the student can see. Say, "I'm going to change *pot* to *not*. Watch."

2. Push the first tile up and say /p/. Push the second tile up and say /o/. Push the third tile up and say /t/. Run your finger under the bottom of the tiles and say the word *pot*. Now touch each tile and say each sound again, /p/ /o/ /t/. Then say, "Watch as I change the first sound /p/ to /n/." Take a new tile that is a different color from the other tiles and use it to push up the first tile. Put the new tile where the old one was and say, "I changed the /p/ to /n/. Doodledeedoo, Sound Switcharoo. *Pot* becomes *not*."

3. Give the student three tiles of the same color. Tell him to put them in a row. Tell the student that the word is *sit*. Have the student push up one tile at a time while he says the phonemes /s/ /i/ /t/. Assist as necessary. Ask the child to point to each tile and say each sound again. Now have the child sweep his finger under the tiles and say, "sit."

4. Explain, "Now you are going to change the first sound in *sit* from /s/ to /b/." Give the child a tile of a different color from his others. Instruct him to use that tile to push up the first tile, placing the new tile where the old one was. Say, "Now you changed the /s/ to /b/. Doodledeedoo, Sound Switcharoo. You made *sit* become *bit*."

5. Tell the student to keep the /b/ /i/ /t/ tiles set up. Instruct him to keep changing the first sound tile to make the following words: *fit, lit, pit,* and *hit*.

6. If the student is struggling, change the segmentation from individual phonemes to onset and rime. In other words, instead of /s/ /i/ /t/, do /s/ /it/ (the student would then use just two tiles).

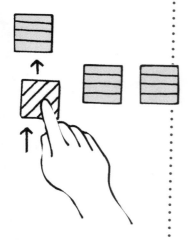

RTI TIER LEVEL

SKILL:
Phoneme
Substitution of
Initial Sound

MATERIALS:
Reproducible
on page 157,
red and green
counters

**LITERATURE
CONNECTION
OPTION**:
*The Substitute
Teacher from the
Black Lagoon*, by
Mike Thaler

Sound Substitute

Directions:

1. Before class, copy and cut out the pictures from the reproducible on page 157.

2. Read *The Substitute Teacher* to the student. Talk about the idea that a substitute replaces the teacher for the day. Discuss other uses of the word *substitute*, such as when mom or dad substitutes or replaces blueberries for strawberries in a recipe.

3. Jokingly say, "Hello, my name is Ms. (or Mr.) Sound Substitute, and I will be the substitute for today. (A disguise is optional.) Your teacher had to go to an important meeting. Today we are going to play a fun word game with counters and pictures."

4. Put down three green counters in a row. Have a red counter nearby. Tell the child to substitute the first green counter with a red one. If the child does that correctly, she is ready to try the picture game.

5. Show her the picture of the pot. Ask the child to identify the picture and the first sound. (pot, /p/) Tell the student that she is going to substitute another sound for the /p/ in *pot* and make a new word. Tell the student to replace the first sound in *pot* with /d/. Ask, "What is the new word?" (dot)

6. If the child struggles, ask her to tell you what the picture word is without the first sound. (She must be able to delete before she can substitute.) If she continues to struggle, use the counters as manipulatives and have them represent the sounds.

7. Stick to the rime /ot/ for several more practice rounds. Ask the student to replace the first sound in *dot* with /l/ (lot); to replace the first sound in *lot* with /n/ (not); and the first sound in *not* with /h/ (hot). Continue with the remaining picture cards and have the student try to make the following sound substitutions:

   ➤ Replace the first sound in *soap* with /r/. (rope)

   ➤ Replace the first sound in *coat* with /b/. (boat)

   ➤ Replace the first sound in *fish* with /d/. (dish)

   ➤ Replace the first sound in *key* with /t/. (tea)

   ➤ Replace the first sound in *dog* with /l/. (log)

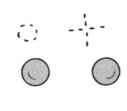

RESOURCES

Important Brain-Based Research for Teachers

The more we understand the brain, the better we'll be able to design instruction to match how it learns best.
—Pat Wolfe, *Brain Matters: Translating Research into Classroom Practice*

The research below was extracted from leading authorities who all share the common belief that effective teachers align their teaching practices with the way the brain learns best. The good news is that you don't have to be a neuroscientist to accomplish this! Infusing the practical applications of these ideas into your daily lessons greatly improves the likelihood that your students will go from passive listeners to actively engaged and motivated learners. You'll find all of the strategies below put into practice throughout this book.

What We Need in the Classroom	Why It's Good for Students' Brains
Music, rhythm, and rhyme	Rhythm and rhyme provide great mechanisms for storing information that would otherwise be difficult to retain. Information embedded in music or rhyme is much easier to recall than the same information in prose (Wolfe 2001).
Movement	Movement integrates and anchors new information and experience into our neural networks. Fully 85 percent of school-age children are kinesthetic learners (Hannaford 1995).
Meaning/Connections	Meaning is more critical to the brain than information (Jensen and Nickelsen 2008). Without offering connections to hook ideas to, many students feel lost or confused by new concepts (Kaufeldt 2005).
Novelty	Novelty is an innate attention-getter (Wolfe 2001). In the brain, novelty stimulates dopamine, which makes you feel good (Feinstein 2004).

What We Need in the Classroom	Why It's Good for Students' Brains
Humor	Humor gives students a "hook" on which to trigger recall (Lundberg and Thurston 2002). Since emotions can enhance retention, laughing will increase the chances of students remembering what they learned. (Kaufeldt 2005).
Enrichment	Two critical ingredients to enrich the learner's brain are challenge and interactive feedback (Jensen 1998). Enriched environments allow the child to be an active participant rather than a passive observer (Diamond and Hopson 1998).
Processing	Without processing information, the brain may remember the information it received incorrectly. It takes more intellectual energy to undo faulty learning than to teach for mastery of the correct information in the first place. (Allen, et al. 2007).
Feedback	Feedback is considered to be the most important ingredient to enhance achievement. The best feedback appears to involve an explanation of what is accurate and what is inaccurate in terms of student responses (Marzano, Pickering, and Pollock 2001).
Multimodal learning	The more pathways you use to input information, the more pathways from which it can be retrieved (Allen, et al. 2007). Each time we add a new way to present the material, the probability of reaching more students increases (Politano and Paquin 2000).
Threat-free environment	The presence of a threat in *any* significant degree impedes learning. One's thinking and learning function only when one feels secure (Sousa 2001).

Study Guide

This study guide is meant to provide you with the opportunity to reflect on your practice and deepen your understanding of phonological awareness (PA) and response to intervention (RTI). It was written so that it can be used by an individual teacher, with small groups, or by entire faculties. The questions focus on PA, RTI, the activities in this book, and assessment.

If you are facilitating a study group or discussing the content of this book as part of a larger professional learning community, you may want to try structuring the questions that follow using one of the ideas listed below.

Partner Share: Divide into groups of four. Within each group of four, divide into pairs. Discuss each question with your partner. Then share with the other pair.

Four Corners: Ask an open-ended question and offer participants four choices. Instruct members of the group to stand in corner 1 if they think/believe _____, corner 2 if they think/believe _____, corner 3 if they think/believe _____, and corner 4 if they think/believe _____. Ask them to discuss with the other people in the group why they chose that corner. As an option, after some discussion time, you may want to invite the people from one of the groups to form a panel in front of the rest of the group. Have the other participants sit down and become the audience. Pretend the panel is a group of visiting experts who will answer questions from the audience.

Mix It with Music: Ask a question. Play some music and have the participants walk around or dance to the music. The facilitator says, "Freeze." Participants partner up with the person standing the closest to them. Partners discuss the question. Invite volunteers to share with the whole group.

Back-to-Back/Celebrate!: This technique is a fun and interactive way to review content. To begin, have all the participants find partners and stand back to back. Ask a question that can be answered by holding up fingers, such as, "How many phonemes in the word *sister*?" or ask a question requiring participants to write a short response on a clipboard, such as "How often do you monitor a tier 2 student?" Each person holds up (or writes) her response, turns around, faces her partner, and shows her answer. If they both have the same response, they celebrate with a high five, fist bump, or celebration of their choice. The facilitator then gives the correct response so that those partners who don't agree know the correct answer. This activity works best when the questions have specific answers.

Response to Intervention

1. At the foundation of response to intervention (RTI) is the need for differentiated instruction (DI). In what ways do you teach now that allow for the diversity in students' backgrounds, skill levels, and interests?

2. Based on your reading of this book as well as other books, what is your understanding of the critical attributes of each of the tiers in the three-tiered RTI model?

3. What do you think are the advantages of the three-tiered RTI model? What might be some obstacles that concern you?

4. Although the classroom teacher represents the first line of early intervention, the RTI model was built with teamwork in mind. It involves collaboration and consultation. Who in your building could be part of the team to observe students, utilize intervention strategies, provide strategies to you, etc.?

5. If you could wave a magic wand, what kind of support would you have in order to successfully implement RTI in your classroom?

6. How are RTI and DI similar? How are they different? Draw a Venn diagram to organize your thoughts.

7. The RTI model requires the use of progress monitoring to inform instruction. How can you use the Phonological Awareness Skills Test (PAST) to strengthen your instruction and improve student achievement?

8. How can you explain to parents that RTI is not "more of the same" general classroom instruction?

9. How would you answer the following questions a parent might have relating to RTI?
   How long will my child remain in a tier before moving to the next tier?
   How often will you monitor my child's progress?
   How will you monitor my child?
   At what point would the school refer my child for an evaluation?

Using the Activities

1. There are 96 activities in this book. How will you decide which to use and when to use them?

2. What strategies in these activities are consistent with your understanding of how the brain learns best?

3. Select a tier 3 activity from this book. List at least two examples of how the instruction is tailored to be more intensive and explicit.

4. How could you modify a tier 1 activity so that it becomes a tier 3 activity? What specifically could you do to make the instruction more intensive and explicit?

5. Have you ever used a story to teach a phonological awareness skill? Why is this a strategy to consider?

6. Do you have a collection of books that use rhyme? How would you go about starting or expanding such a collection? Who could help you?

7. What helpful and encouraging response would you give to a teacher who says, "I can't do these activities because I don't have the time"?

8. How would you respond to a tier 3 student who asks, "Why am I working with you alone?"

9. What are some quick phonological awareness activities parents can do at home with their child that require little or no preparation and materials?

10. If you are working on phonological awareness skills with a professional learning community, consider trying the following role-play activity:

    In groups of four, assign each member a number from one to four. Number 1 will play the role of the teacher. Number 2 will play the role of the student. Numbers 3 and 4 are the coaches. The facilitator chooses a tier 3 activity from this book. Give the "teacher" about three to five minutes to do part of that activity with the "student." Numbers 3 and 4 observe. (The other groups in the room are simultaneously doing the same thing.) After five minutes, the facilitator rings a bell and all groups stop. The coaches share their observations. Next time, switch roles so that the coaches become the teacher and student, and the other two participants become the coaches.

Assessment

1. How can the Phonological Awareness Skills Test (PAST) included in this book help with RTI and the data-driven decision-making process?

2. How do you currently assess your students' PA skills? How do you use the data? Does the data inform your teaching? How often do you monitor your students?

3. How can you use the PAST as a tool for continuous progress monitoring? How can it be used to strengthen your instruction and improve student achievement?

4. Consider administering the PAST to a colleague before you administer it to children. What did you learn? Did anything surprise you? Would you alter any of it when administering it to your students? Why?

5. What additional information do you think you might get about a student if you administer the PAST, as compared to asking a paraprofessional or other teacher to administer it?

6. When and how might you share a PAST Student Progress Report with a parent?

7. If you have Spanish-speaking children in your school who do not yet speak English, is there anyone at your school who could administer the Spanish-language PAST to those children?

8. Research shows that phonological awareness skills transfer from one language to another (Durgunoglu and Oney 2000). If a Spanish-speaking student has a poor sense of phonological awareness in his native language, what suggestions could you offer to the child's parents?

9. What helpful and encouraging response would you give to a teacher who says, "I can't use the PAST because I don't have the time."?

Interventions for All: Phonological Awareness

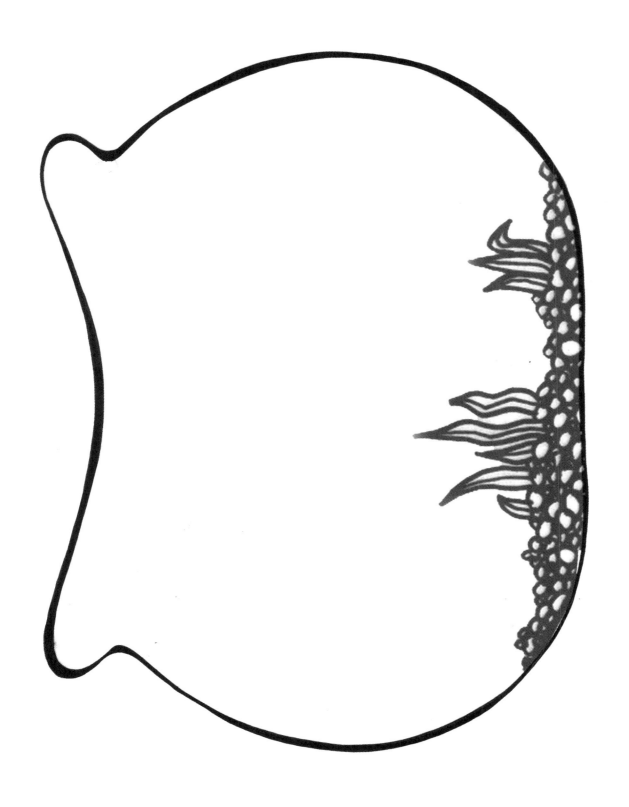

Use with Disappearing Goldfish, page 53.

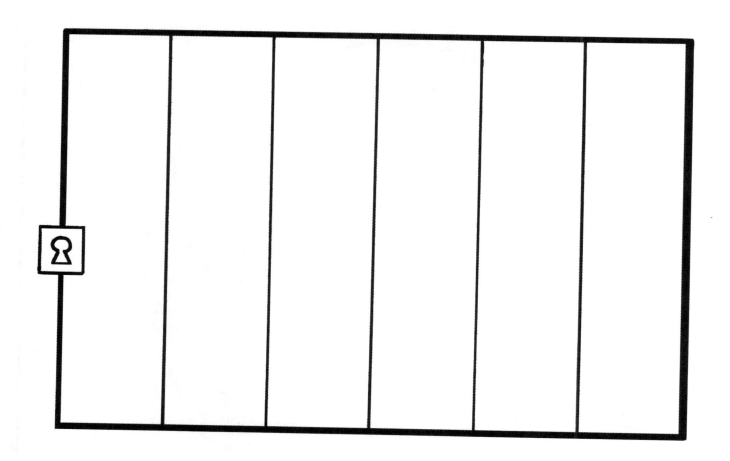

Use with Rhymenappers, page 60.

Interventions for All: Phonological Awareness

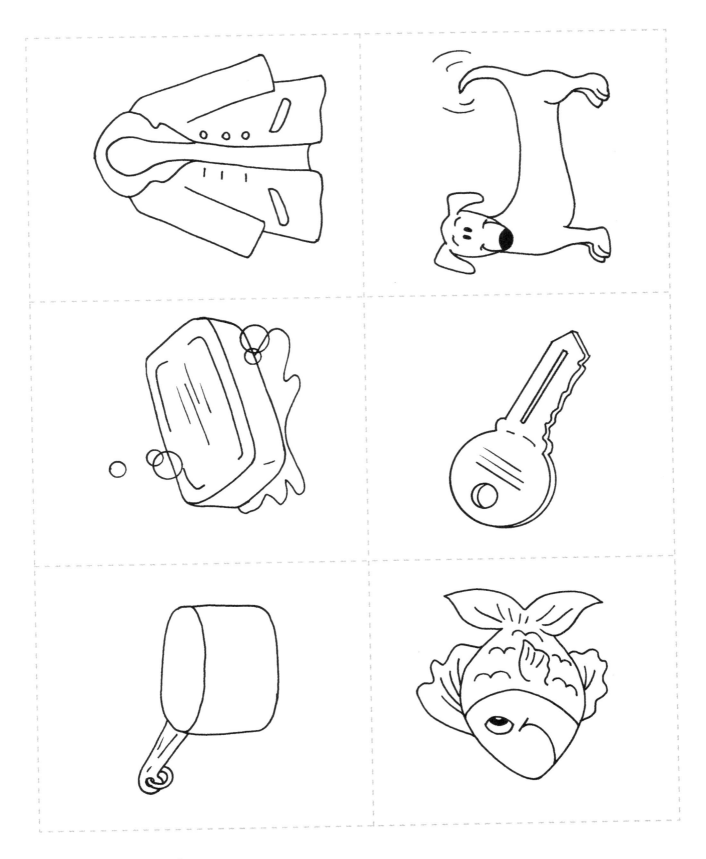

pot, soap, coat, fish, key, dog

Use with I'm Thinking of a Word, page 66, Stretch It Out, page 108, and Sound Substitute, page 145.

cup, dime, hand, cake, flag, mop, plane, sock, tent

Use with Rhymo! page 72, Pop-Up Sound Sort, page 120 and Sound Off!, page 124.

Interventions for All: Phonological Awareness

Use with Make It Go!, page 78.

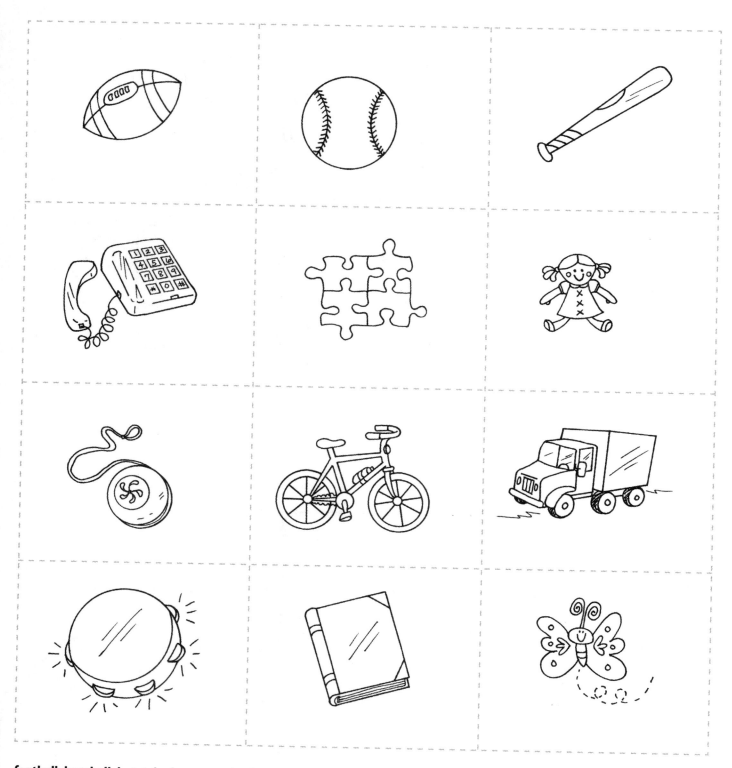

football, baseball, bat, telephone, puzzle, doll, yo-yo, bicycle, truck, tambourine, book, butterfly

Use with We're Going to the Toy Store, page 82, and Syllable Sort, page 84.

Interventions for All: Phonological Awareness

umbrella, popsicle, elephant, banana, ring, watermelon, cookie, apple, carrot, tomato, frog, kangaroo

Use with Walking 100 Syllables, page 83.

cowboy, toenail, rainbow, cupcake, basketball, doorbell

Directions: Cut out each flip book. Then cut up the middle line to the X.

Use with Hide-Away Syllables, page 90.

Interventions for All: Phonological Awareness   REPRODUCIBLE

boat, house, lamp, corn, pail, fork, leaf, nest, pig

Use with Beanbag Toss, page 100, and Turn Man Into Pan, page 140.

Use with Conductor School, page 119, and Sound Cuts, page 131.

Interventions for All: Phonological Awareness   REPRODUCIBLE

Use with Unflatten Flat Stanley, page 117.

Children's Books Used in the Activities

100th Day Worries, by Margery Cuyler

Bringing the Rain to Kapiti Plain, by Verna Aardema

Brown Bear, Brown Bear, What Do You See?, by Bill Martin Jr.

Check It Out! The Book About Libraries, by Gail Gibbons

Chrysanthemum, by Kevin Henkes

Diary of a Worm, by Doreen Cronin

Flat Stanley, by Jeff Brown

Fly Away Home, by Eve Bunting

The Fourth Little Pig, by Teresa Celsi

Franny B. Kranny, There's a Bird in Your Hair!, by Harriet Lerner & Susan Goldhor

Freight Train, by Donald Crews

Germs Make Me Sick!, by Melvin Berger

The Great Kapok Tree, by Lynne Cherry

Hey, Little Ant, by Phillip & Hannah Hoose

Hooray for Diffendoofer Day!, by Dr. Suess, Jack Prelutsky & Lane Smith

The Hungry Thing, by Jan Slepian & Jan Seidler

The Important Book, by Margaret Wise Brown

Ira Sleeps Over, by Bernard Waber

The Kissing Hand, by Audrey Penn

Lilly's Purple Plastic Purse, by Kevin Henkes

The Little Engine That Could, by Watty Piper

Madeline, by Ludwig Bemelmans

The Magic School Bus At the Waterworks, by Joanna Cole

The Magic School Bus Inside the Human Body, by Joanna Cole

Make Way for Ducklings, by Robert McCloskey

The Memory String, by Eve Bunting

Miss Nelson Is Missing!, by James Marshall

Oh, How I Wished I Could Read!, by John Gile

Oliver Button Is a Sissy, by Tomie dePaola

One Fish Two Fish Red Fish Blue Fish, by Dr. Suess

A Picture Book of Anne Frank, by David Adler

The Relatives Came, by Cynthia Rylant

Rhyming Dust Bunnies, by Jan Thomas

The Royal Bee, by Frances Park & Ginger Park

Sharks, by Gail Gibbons

The Snowy Day, by Ezra Jack Keats

So Many Circles, So Many Squares, by Tana Hoban

Spiders, by Gail Gibbons

Stellaluna, by Janell Cannon

Stranger in the Woods: A Photographic Fantasy, by Carl R. Sams II & Jean Stoick

The Substitute Teacher from the Black Lagoon, by Mike Thaler

The Teacher from the Black Lagoon, by Mike Thaler

The Umbrella, by Jan Brett

The Very Hungry Caterpillar, by Eric Carle

WBUG Radio Up Close and Personal: An Interview with Harry the Tarantula, by Leigh Ann Tyson

When the Teacher Isn't Looking And Other Funny School Poems, by Kenn Nesbitt

Why Do Dogs Bark?, by Joan Holub

Zoo-Looking, by Mem Fox

References and Suggested Readings

Adams, M.J. 1990. *Beginning to Read: Thinking and Learning about Print*. Cambridge, MA: MIT Press.

Adams, M.J., B. Foorman, I. Lundberg, and T. Beeler. 1998. *Phonemic Awareness in Young Children*. Baltimore, MD: Paul H. Brookes Publishing Co.

Allen, L., L. Nickelsen, and Y. Zgonc. 2007. *Prepping the Brain: Easy and Effective Ways to Get Kids Ready for Learning*. Peterborough, NH: Crystal Springs Books.

Armbruster, B., F. Lehr, and J. Osborn. 2001. *Put Reading First: The Research Building Blocks for Teaching Children to Read*. Partnership for Reading, www.nifl.gov/partnershipforreading.

Ball, E.W., and B.A. Blachman. 1991. Does phoneme awareness training in kindergarten make a difference in early word recognition and developmental spelling? *Reading Research Quarterly*, 26 (1), 49–66.

Beninghof, A.M. 2006. *Engage All Students Through Differentiation*. Peterborough, NH: Crystal Springs Books.

Blachman, B., E. Ball, R. Black, and D. Tangel. 2000. *Road to the Code: A Phonological Awareness Program for Young Children*. Baltimore, MD: Paul H. Brookes Publishing Co.

Blevins, W. 1997. *Phonemic Awareness Activities for Early Reading Success*. New York: Scholastic Inc.

Byrne, B., and R. Fielding-Barnsley. 1991. Evaluation of a program to teach phonemic awareness to young children. *Journal of Educational Psychology*, 83, 451–455.

———. 1993. Evaluation of a program to teach phonemic awareness to young children: A 1-year follow-up. *Journal of Educational Psychology*, 85, 104–111.

———. 1995. Evaluation of a program to teach phonemic awareness to young children: A 2- and 3-year follow-up and a new preschool trial. *Journal of Educational Psychology*, 8, 488–503.

Davis, K. 2000. *Phonemic Awareness: "Hear It and Say It" with Frog Street Friends!* Crandall, TX: Frog Street Press.

Diamond, M., and J. Hopson. 1998. *Magic Trees of the Mind: How to Nurture Your Child's Intelligence, Creativity, and Healthy Emotions from Birth Through Adolescence*. New York: Penguin Putnam, Inc.

Durgunoglu, A., and B. Oney. 2000. *Literacy Development in two languages: Cognitive and sociocultural dimensions of cross-language transfer*. In a Research Symposium on High Standards in Reading for Students from Diverse Language Groups: Research, Practice & Policy, 78–99. Washington, DC: U.S. Department of Education, Office of Bilingual Education and Minority Languages Affairs, www.ncela.gwu.edu/pubs/symposia/reading/index.htm.

Ehri, L.C., S.R. Nunes, D.M. Willows, B.V. Schuster, Z. Yaghoub-Zadeh, and T. Shanahan. 2001. Phonemic awareness instruction helps children learn to read: Evidence from the National Reading Panel's meta-analysis. *Reading Research Quarterly* 36 (3): 250–287.

Feinstein, S. 2004. *Secrets of the Teenage Brain*. San Diego, CA: The Brain Store.

Fitzpatrick, J. 1997. *Phonemic Awareness: Playing with Sounds to Strengthen Beginning Reading Skills.* Cypress, CA: Creative Teaching Press.

Glynn, Carol. 2001. *Learning on Their Feet: A Sourcebook for Kinesthetic Learning Across the Curriculum K–8.* Shoreham, VT: Discover Writing Press.

Goldsworthy, C.L. 1998. *Sourcebook of Phonological Awareness Activities: Children's Classic Literature.* San Diego, CA: Singular Publishing Group, Inc.

Goodman, G. 2008. *Interventions for Struggling Learners: Putting RTI Into Practice.* Peterborough, NH: Crystal Springs Books.

Haager, D., J.A. Dimino, and M.P. Windmueller. 2007. *Interventions for Reading Success.* Baltimore, MD: Paul H. Brookes Publishing Co.

Hall, S.L. 2008. *Implementing Response to Intervention: A Principal's Guide.* Thousand Oaks, CA: Corwin Press, Inc.

Hannaford, C. 1995. *Smart Moves: Why Learning Is Not All in Your Head.* Arlington, VA: Great Ocean Publishers.

Jensen, E. 1998. *Teaching with the Brain in Mind.* Alexandria, VA: Association for Supervision and Curriculum Development.

Jensen, E., and L. Nickelsen. 2008. *Deeper Learning: 7 Powerful Strategies for In-Depth and Longer-Lasting Learning.* Thousand Oaks, CA: Corwin Press.

Jordano, K., and T. Callella-Jones. 1998. *Phonemic Awareness Songs & Rhymes:* Cypress, CA: Creative Teaching Press, Inc. (This series includes three books: one each for winter, spring, and fall.)

Kaufeldt, M. 2005. *Teachers, Change Your Bait: Brain-Compatible Differentiated Instruction.* Norwalk, CT: Crown House Publishing Ltd.

Kemp, K., and M.A. Eaton. 2008. *RTI: The Classroom Connection for Literacy.* Port Chester, NY: Dude Publishing.

Lundberg, E., and C.M. Thurston. 2002. *If They're Laughing, They Just Might Be Listening.* Fort Collins, CO: Cottonwood Press, Inc.

Marzano, R.J., D.J. Pickering, and J.E. Pollock. 2001. *Classroom Instruction that Works: Research-Based Strategies for Increasing Student Achievement.* Alexandria, VA: Association for Supervision and Curriculum Development.

Medina, J. 2008. *Brain Rules.* Seattle, WA: Pear Press.

Nichols, C. (Project Editor). 2002. *Evidence-Based Reading Instruction: Putting the National Reading Panel Report Into Practice.* Newark, DE: International Reading Association.

O'Connor, R.E., J.R. Jenkins, N. Leicester, and T.A. Slocum. 1993. Teaching phonological awareness to young children with learning disabilities. *Exceptional Children* 59 (6): 532–546.

Politano, C., and J. Paquin. 2000. *Brain-Based Learning With Class.* Winnipeg, Canada: Portage & Main Press.

Ratey, J.J., with E. Hagerman. 2008. *Spark: The Revolutionary New Science of Exercise and the Brain.* Park Avenue, NY: Little, Brown and Company.

Sousa, D.A. 2001. *How the Brain Learns.* (2nd ed.) Thousand Oaks, CA: Corwin Press, Inc.

Sprenger, M. 2002. *Becoming a "Wiz" at Brain-Based Teaching.* Thousand Oaks, CA: Corwin Press, Inc.

Wolfe, P. 2001. *Brain Matters: Translating Research into Classroom Practice.* Alexandria, VA: Association for Supervision and Curriculum Development.

Wolfe, P., and P. Nevills. 2004. *Building the Reading Brain, PreK–3.* Thousand Oaks, CA: Corwin Press, Inc.

Yopp, H.K., and L. Stapleton. 2008. Conciencia fonémica en español (Phonemic Awareness in Spanish). *The Reading Teacher* 61 (5): 374–382.

Yopp, H.K., and R.H. Yopp. 2000. Supporting phonemic awareness development in the classroom. *The Reading Teacher* 54 (2): 130–143.

———. 2002. *Oo-pples and boo-noo-noo: Songs and Activities for Phonemic Awareness.* (2nd ed.) Orlando, FL: Harcourt School Publishers.

Zgonc, Y. 2000. *Sounds in Action: Phonological Awareness Activities & Assessment.* Peterborough, NH: Crystal Springs Books.

Index

Note: Page Numbers in italics indicate reproducibles.

NOTES

NOTES

NOTES

NOTES

NOTES